The Talk

Sharon Maxwell, Ph.D.

The Talk

what your **kids**

need to hear from

you about sex

avery • *a member of penguin group (usa) inc.* • new york

Published by the Penguin Group
Penguin Group (USA) Inc., 375 Hudson Street, New York, New York 10014, USA ·
Penguin Group (Canada), 90 Eglinton Avenue East, Suite 700, Toronto, Ontario M4P 2Y3,
Canada (a division of Pearson Canada Inc.) · Penguin Books Ltd, 80 Strand,
London WC2R 0RL, England · Penguin Ireland, 25 St Stephen's Green, Dublin 2, Ireland
(a division of Penguin Books Ltd) · Penguin Group (Australia), 250 Camberwell Road, Camberwell,
Victoria 3124, Australia (a division of Pearson Australia Group Pty Ltd) ·
Penguin Books India Pvt Ltd, 11 Community Centre, Panchsheel Park, New Delhi–110 017,
India · Penguin Group (NZ), 67 Apollo Drive, Rosedale, North Shore 0632, New Zealand
(a division of Pearson New Zealand Ltd) · Penguin Books (South Africa) (Pty) Ltd, 24 Sturdee Avenue,
Rosebank, Johannesburg 2196, South Africa

Penguin Books Ltd, Registered Offices: 80 Strand, London WC2R 0RL, England

Most Avery books are available at special quantity discounts for bulk purchase for sales promotions,
premiums, fund-raising, and educational needs. Special books or book excerpts also can be created to fit
specific needs. For details, write Penguin Group (USA) Inc. Special Markets, 375 Hudson Street, New
York, NY 10014.

Library of Congress Cataloging-in-Publication Data
Maxwell, Sharon.
The talk : what your kids need to hear from you about sex / Sharon Maxwell.
p.   cm.
ISBN 978-1-58333-310-5
1. Sex instruction for children.   2. Sex instruction for youth.   3. Sex instruction for children—
Religious aspects.   4. Parent and child.   I. Title.
HQ57.M385   2008   2008005259
649'.65—dc22

Printed in the United States of America
1   3   5   7   9   10   8   6   4   2

BOOK DESIGN BY NICOLE LAROCHE

While the author has made every effort to provide accurate telephone numbers and Internet addresses at
the time of publication, neither the publisher nor the author assumes any responsibility for errors, or for
changes that occur after publication. Further, the publisher does not have any control over and does not
assume any responsibility for author or third-party websites or their content.

Neither the publisher nor the author is engaged in rendering professional advice or services to the individual reader. The ideas, procedures, and suggestions contained in this book are not intended as a substitute
for consulting with your physician. All matters regarding your health require medical supervision. Neither
the author nor the publisher shall be liable or responsible for any loss or damage allegedly arising from any
information or suggestion in this book.

author's note

• •

The stories in this book come from my clinical practice, my work-shops for parents, educators, and health professionals, the class-room, and from parenting my own teens. The names, places, and details have been altered such that they no longer resemble any particular person. Any similarity between the names and stories of individuals described in this book and anyone known to readers is inadvertent and purely coincidental.

acknowledgments

· ·

barbara Smith Decker believed in this book. A great friend and professional editor, she became my writing coach. Throughout this process she brought clarity, skill, and much needed encouragement. For every moment of your precious time and all those cold winter nights in my basement, I thank you, Barbara, with all my heart.

To all the young people I have known and worked with, my deepest gratitude. The people I refer to in the book are not you, but fabricated combinations of the hopes and dreams and confusions that all of you have brought to me over the years, both in my office and in the classroom. Working with each one of you has been an honor. This book is my way of trying to shake things up. I wish for each of you the freedom and discipline to offer the best of who you are to a world that very much needs your unique passion and intelligence.

Deep thanks to Rabbi Starr, Pastor Jim, and all the spiritual teachers I have had the great good fortune to learn from over the years. You have inspired me with your wisdom and profound love and commitment to children and families.

My agent, Faith Hamlin, "got it" and in one moment I knew this book would happen. Faith, you must be the most patient, even-tempered person in the world. What a great gift you have been to me and to any writer who has the opportunity to work with you. A special thanks to Courtney Miller-Callihan, who answered all my calls and questions with serenity, encouragement, and enthusiasm.

Much gratitude to the great team at Penguin: Megan Newman, Miriam Rich, Kate Stark, Anne Kosmoski, and Rebecca Behan. It's a strange thing to hand your book to someone and hold your breath while it tumbles around. At some point, the book comes into focus again but it's subtly different and amazingly better. It's quite magical and, in the end, wonderful.

When my daughter was two, Eric and I decided to relocate to Massachusetts because we couldn't imagine how we would raise healthy children without extended family. We also had no idea how hard it would be to restart two professional careers in our forties. Thank you, Eric, for always putting family first, whatever the cost.

My sister, Carla, is my best friend and constant source of love and support. Her honesty and encouragement are invaluable.

My dad's unconditional love is the foundation for everything I accomplish. He models a life lived with absolute confidence that anything is possible with enough effort, perseverance, and grace. Thank you, Dad.

Every daughter carries within her the spirit of her mom. If my words can express even a fraction of what my mom knew, I will be very, very happy.

My Dear Ones,

It isn't easy having a mom who goes around talking about sex, yet together you have supported me with an abundance of humor, grace, and intelligence. I am so grateful for your love. It gives each moment purpose and fills me with hope and joy.

contents

• • • • • • • • • • • • • • • • • • • •

Who I Am and What This Book Is About

Dear Reader,

An incident on a school playground changed my career and how I understood my job as a mother. Someone else was teaching my seven-year-old about sex, and I wanted it to be me.

As a clinical psychologist for more than ten years I had specialized in and loved working with adolescents and families, but my first job and great passion was mothering. Doing my part in raising the next generation of human beings, providing them with an environment that nurtured whatever unique contribution they would make to the world, defined and continues to define my life. Perhaps it's because I waited so long to have children, or because it almost didn't happen. For whatever reason, like so many parents before me, life acquired meaning and purpose beyond anything I had ever known when I became a mom.

Most of us who take on the job of parenting have a moment in time when we realize that despite our most diligent efforts, our children will be profoundly influenced by factors outside of our control. It might be the first time we put them on the school bus, listen to their sadness and confusion at being rejected by another child, or are taken aback by something they say that we know they didn't learn at home. There is a moment of shock as we realize that our children's understanding of the world and of themselves will be fashioned by experiences outside of our control, that our influence is limited and will continue to diminish with every passing year. Logically we understand that this is as it should be, yet we can't help but question whether we have sufficiently prepared them for the world they will encounter.

That moment with my son made it clear to me. When it came to issues of sexuality, not only had I not prepared my son and daughter for a world that was constantly selling sex in a manner that was far from inspiring, but I had not really thought through where I stood with regard to sexuality or how I would want them to understand this important part of their development.

In my private practice I see the impact of the media on teens' sexual attitudes, as well as how unaware most parents are when it comes to understanding how kids are thinking about sex. If I were going to adequately prepare my own children for adolescence I needed to figure out where I stood with regard to sexuality and develop a language to begin that conversation now. My daughter was nine, my son seven.

Already a lecturer on issues of parenting, I began to develop parent workshops on healthy ways of discussing sex with kids. These talks developed into a series of articles for a parenting magazine that led to a national Parenting Publications of America award. The curriculum director for a public school system asked me to develop a sex education curriculum for fifth graders. What a gift that was! I was able to really look at how schools talk to our kids about sex and I found a great deal missing.

Helping kids see how the media influences their understanding of sexuality was missing, a critical oversight in a day and age where most kids learn about how to act sexually from the media. No one was talking to kids about the value of self-discipline: developing the internal muscle to say no to something that feels good is an essential tool in becoming a responsible sexual person. Most importantly, the parents were missing. While schools give information, parents set ethical guidelines for behavior. When it comes to sex, both are needed.

My passion turned to developing a curriculum that gave kids information about sex and included issues like media manipulation of sexual desire and the importance of developing the muscle of self-discipline. Most important, it included parents by showing them how to think through their values with regard to sexuality so that they could continue the conversation at home. Working directly with kids in the classroom as well as with parents and health teachers has been invaluable in continually making this work relevant to the day-to-day realities of families.

As this curriculum became recognized I got calls from religious institutions. Rabbis, priests, and ministers from both conservative and liberal denominations were interested in using my approach to sexuality to address parents and teens in their communities. Each opportunity I've had to work with a religious leader has profoundly enriched my understanding of sexuality. Our discussions have enhanced my ability to talk about sex in a way that inspired interest in understanding the responsibility we each have to use our sexuality in an ethical way.

As I spoke with more and more parents, it became clear that technology and the clash of cultural and family values presented unique challenges for moms and dads of children of all ages. Parents of younger children are looking for ways to set reasonable guidelines for all forms of media; parents of older children are concerned with how the Internet impacts their kids' sexual development; mothers want workshops that address issues specific to empowering girls as they navigate the challenges of adolescence.

Each of these interests has turned into workshops, articles, and, ultimately, the chapters of this book.

I have a great suspicion of parenting books. Too often I see parents give up their common sense attempting to try something some "expert" says is the right thing to do. Don't use this book that way! Each of you knows more about sex than I could ever tell you. You have that amazing love for your child that will guide you to say the right thing, at the right time. Let the ideas in this book stir up your thinking about sex, about our culture, and about what you want for your child. Talk to your partner or friends. Form a parenting group at your child's school, church, or synagogue. I would love to hear from you and know what works and what doesn't.

It is a great gift to be able to turn one's passion into one's work. My passion comes from wanting to be the best mother I can be. I am incredibly grateful to be able to use my education and professional experience to turn that passion into an offering for families.

SHARON MAXWELL, PH.D.
DrSharonMaxwell.com

· · · · · · · · · · · · · · · ·

one

It's Personal and the Stakes Are High

mom, do you know what a stripper and a hooker are?" It's 1998, my son is seven years old, and I'm driving him home from school. He's in second grade. Perhaps the question shouldn't have been such a shock, but I'm the kind of mother that every kid dreads having, the kind who knows everything they've ever watched on TV, who doesn't allow any video-game players in the house, who even refused to shell out money for a pack of Pokémon cards when having a social life demanded something expensive to trade on the playground. So where on earth had he heard about strippers and hookers? Realizing that I was about to blow an important moment with a semihysterical response, I took a deep breath and calmly replied in my best therapist voice, "Yes, I know what a stripper and a hooker are. Do you?"

"Yes," he replies. "A stripper is a girl who takes off her top and a hooker is when she takes everything off."

I did a lot of deep breathing that day.

The story began at recess when my son's classmate, another seven-year-old, told a group of boys about a video game that he had played at a twelve-year-old neighbor's house. The game goes like this: If you kill a lot of people and make it to a certain level, you enter a room where a "stripper" takes off her top. If you kill more people and get to a higher level, you go to a room where a woman takes off all her clothes. According to my son, that's what you call a "hooker." The name of this game is Duke Nukem, available for rental in video stores. It gets worse. When I related this story during one of my first parent workshops, a mother in the audience asked me if I knew what happened if you killed everyone and made it to the highest level of this game. She knew because she had walked in on her seventeen-year-old playing it: the ultimate reward is entrée into a room full of naked women hanging off meat hooks.[1]

Back in the car, I listen to my son's thoughts about this game. I tell him that I don't think this is a good game, that putting naked ladies and killing people together and making it a reward is wrong. As I talk, I try to put myself in his head. I'm aware that the camaraderie of boys all sharing a secret has been stimulating. He has no context for understanding why naked ladies would be a reward for anything and he's trying to make sense of it. If I don't step in and give him some kind of context for all of this, someone else will.

Someone already has excited his interest. My son, at seven, has a category in his brain where sex and violence are now connected, where women's bodies are viewed as a commodity that violent men are entitled to. But what most infuriates me is that a piece of my parenting has been taken away. Someone has stolen my right to be the first person to explain the profoundly beautiful aspects of human sexuality. Hearing a story like this, it's natural to want to find a bad guy, someone to blame, a really rotten parent indifferent to their child's welfare, messing things up for the rest of us.

I call the little boy's mother. She is horrified. She had given explicit instructions to the parents of the twelve-year-old that her son was not allowed to play video games at their house. She hadn't done anything wrong. Upset, she calls the twelve-year-old's parents. But there were no bad parents there, either. They were caring and concerned parents, mortified about what had happened. Both were professional educators who had never heard of Duke Nukem. Their son rented the game at a local video store. Did they drop the ball? Yes, by not examining what he was renting. Yet in their defense, they were completely unaware that a game like that even existed. Launching a one-woman campaign against this game, I found it in every video store in my area.

But I couldn't find any irresponsible parents in this story, just caring—but clueless—parents working hard to create the best environment they can for their kids. Good parents like myself who, short of moving into a cave or joining the Amish, could not keep our children from being inundated with sexually explicit material at a very young age.

So as parents, what can we do? How do we hold on to our right to raise our children with the values and attitudes we believe in, in a world that is deluging them with a very different view of reality?

We begin to think and act proactively. We wake up to the reality that the whole world is talking to our kids about sex—and it is our job to find a language to begin this conversation at an early age and sustain a dialogue with them about sex until we send them off to college. If we don't get there first, someone will rob us of our right to raise children who can become healthy, responsible sexual adults. So where do we start?

First, let's open our eyes to the attitudes and assumptions about sex and sexuality that are all around us and how they are changing our children's understanding of their sexuality. We are so used to being saturated in sexual humor and innuendo and visually bombarded with explicit sexual material that we don't really see it anymore. Yes, Duke Nukem is a dramatic and disturbing example of how children can be needlessly exposed to demeaning and violent sex. But the more pervasive, subtle messages can have even greater impact on how our children understand their sexuality and learn to make sexual choices.

Look at the random sample of headlines from women's magazines at the checkout stand of a local supermarket.

"405 Ways to Look Hot at Every Party," *Seventeen*

"30 Red-Hot Sex Secrets," *Men's Health*

"SEX GOSSIP: Tips and Tricks only Your Friends Will Tell You," *Redbook*

"Real Women Confess Their Sex Fantasies," *Glamour*

One of the most dangerous things parents can do is assume that their children are not seeing or thinking about the sexually stimulating material around them. Parents will very often tell me, "Oh, he doesn't see that stuff. That just passes right over his head."

WRONG.

Kids see it all and they are making assumptions about what is "normal" and "expected" from what they see.

When my daughter was eleven years old, I saw her reading this headline from a popular women's magazine as we were standing in line to buy groceries: "10 DATES BEFORE SEX??! & Other Secrets of Love That Lasts and Lasts."

"What do you think that means?" I asked her. She thought for a while and then said, "I guess it means that ten dates is how long you wait before you have sex."

Our children build their understanding about what sex is and how they are supposed to be as sexual people from sources that have no concern for their well-being and no interest in the social/sexual values they are forming. Our children want our guidance as to how responsible men and woman are supposed to use their sexuality. They want to know where we stand when it comes to using sex to acquire power and social status.

Starting these conversations is not easy. Most of us were left to figure sex out for ourselves. We are at a loss, not only about how and when to start the conversation but as our children get older, what kind of advice we want to give that will guide them through middle school, high school, and college and into adulthood. Dive in anyway. No matter how badly you botch it, you're bound to be better than Duke Nukem or MTV.

Media Manipulation for Fun and Profit

In pursuit of a face to put behind Duke Nukem, I came upon this quote by George Broussard, cofounder of 3D Realms, which makes the game: "Duke is a mass-market character that can sell 2 million games. It'd be suicide to make the game unplayable by younger people."[2]

Parents have to understand that in the grand scheme of American commerce, filling little boys' minds with pictures of women hanging off meat hooks as a reward for killing is *not a consideration*. There are no rules. In fact, at a time when parents have less and less time with their children, there is a universe of advertisers ready to fill the gap.

Children in America influence the spending of more than $500 billion a year.[3] That kind of money makes corporate America take notice. "When marketers think of kids, they should think of KIDS—Keepers of Infinite Dollars," writes Texas A&M marketing professor James McNeal in his book *The Kids Market: Myths and Realities*.

What is it worth to get a child to recognize a corporate logo or feel that having a particular product will make him or her happy and popular? For corporate America today, about $15 billion a year.[4] By capturing our children's attention, marketers not only direct billions of consumer dollars today, but can begin to direct their spending for life.

As one General Mills executive put it, "When it comes to targeting kid consumers, we at General Mills follow the Procter & Gamble model of 'cradle to grave'; we believe in getting them early and having them for life."[5]

Parents need to know that not only are great sums of money being spent to get our children to want a particular product, but also the way in which advertisers target children affects how our children feel about themselves and the world they live in. Professionals trained in the vulnerabilities of children at different developmental stages have been designing ads that play on children's weaknesses for decades.[6] As advertising executive Nancy Shalek of the Shalek Agency put it nearly twenty years ago: "Advertising at its best is making people feel that—without their product—you're a loser. Kids are very sensitive to that. If you tell them to buy something, they are resistant. But if you tell them that they'll be a dork if they don't, you've got their attention. You open up emotional vulnerabilities—and that's very easy to do with kids because they're the most emotionally vulnerable."[7]

Every parent who puts a TV set in his or her child's bedroom (as do 68 percent of parents of children over eight years old[8]) should let the power of that quote really sink in. Corporate America will use all the psychological techniques at their disposal, including undermining children's self-worth, to sell their products. So what does this have to do with raising sexually responsible children? If you're an advertiser and your only goal is to capture the attention of an eleven-year-old, what do you do? How do you play on the emotional vulnerabilities of that child?

First, you tantalize them with a very exciting, grown-up world that they are not supposed to know about. The defining element of that world is sex, so you hint at, construct humor around, and make reference to sex as often as possible. You create television shows about high school kids. You hire drop-dead gorgeous actors and actresses in their twenties to play these high school students and have them dress and act in ways that make it clear that sexy is not only way cool, but very socially powerful. You reinforce the "us against the world" mentality that is so much a part of a teen's development by making sure the grown-ups are either clueless or absurdly selfish, leaving the "teens" in the show with only each other to rely on. Your ratings stay at the top by constantly pushing the envelope with references to sexual behavior that a generation ago would have been relegated to porn movies, supporting a "plot" that spins around who is having sex with whom. Throughout the show, you weave in a steady stream of current pop music that kids can download on their iPods and turn into ringtones on their cell phones, reinforcing how young viewers can belong to the teen culture created by that show. And finally we get to the real plot. During the commercial breaks, you pitch acne creams, hair products, over-the-counter diet regimes, and Snickers bars. And you pitch them in a way that lets children know that without these products, they could become losers, nerds, pimple-infested, perpetually-bad-hair-day teens who would never make it in the supercool television world they are watching. This is average evening fare for millions of American children.

Each generation defines itself in its adolescence. Every generation develops its own style of dress, slang, attitude, and, of course, music. Identifying with peer culture—rather than family culture—is the way teens muster the strength to leave home. But our children's generation is not defining itself: its identity is being defined and manipulated by corporations that have perfected the art of selling to the insecurities of adolescents.[9]

• •

take it home

Make a date with your partner to watch a television program targeted to teens. Pretend that you are not parents, but rather you are aliens from another planet and you are trying to decide what human beings are like based on this show, including all commercials. As you are watching, think about these questions:

- How are young females supposed to act in order to gain status among their peers?
- How are young males expected to act?
- How is it that humans decide when to have sex?
- How do they decide with whom to have sex?
- Why do people have sex in this civilization?

• •

Have Things Really Changed That Much?

Haven't teens always pushed the sexual envelope? Didn't we all go through a time of sexual exploration and survive without much guidance from our parents? Yes. And we must ask how this failure to give guidance, to address one of the most important aspects of human development, the responsible use of one's sexuality, has contributed to confusing and stressful family environments our children are growing up in. With more than a quarter of our children living in single-family homes[10] and a divorce rate just under 50 percent,[11] and the ever-looming threat of AIDS, how can we not try to do a better job than our parents in addressing responsible sexual behavior. We can decide that this generation of teens will be sent off to college with some real guidelines about how to be a sexually responsible person, how to love and respect themselves, and how to intelligently pick a life partner who will love and respect them.

We begin by addressing why our children are adopting an attitude of sexy before they've even reached puberty; exploring kinds of sexual behavior that have always been associated with more mature sexual relationships; and, most important, are not thinking about sex as an act of intimacy and relationship but as a commodity.

We have all read the news reports of kids, middle school age, having oral sex on school buses, in movie theaters, and in school bathrooms. A father recently told me of a game played at a bar mitzvah party where boys formed a circle around the girls and threw a ten-dollar bill into the circle. The girl who picked up the bill would go "do it" with the boy in the coatroom. In a report released by the National Center for Health Statistics in 2005, 54 percent of boys and 53 percent of girls ages fifteen to nineteen were engaging in oral sex. Kids don't think that oral sex is sex—and they do not think that having oral sex puts them at risk for sexually transmitted diseases, including AIDS. Of course, all of this does not mean that your teen, or any of their friends, is having oral sex. It *does* mean that this is the world our children are living in and we all need to be proactive and start talking.

At a recent middle school parent presentation, a father challenged my assertions that it was important for parents to talk to their kids about sex, specifically oral sex. He was sure this was just more media hype and that "this kind of thing" was not happening in his community. A woman in the back of the auditorium raised her hand.

"I'm a nurse in this town," she announced. "Would you like to hear about the number of teens I treated for oral gonorrhea this week?"

A mother stood up. "My son, on his first day of middle school, had an eighth-grade girl walk up to him in the lobby and offer him a blow job. When he got in the car after school I had to tell him what a blow job was."

The difference with regard to sex between this generation and ours is not just oral sex. Having authored and taught sexual health and responsibility curriculums to thousands of fifth and sixth graders it became clear early on that all questions have to be submitted in writing because questions like, "What is anal sex?" "What is a threesome?" and "Do people really have sex with animals?" are not unusual in a class for ten- and eleven-year-olds. While it is natural for children to show sexual curiosity, the content of their questions and the anxiety with which they ask them reveal the pressure they feel to understand the hypersexualized world they've grown up in.

Six-year-olds are "shaking their booty," begging for pants that say "Juicy" on their butts, and singing "I'm too sexy for my shirt." Children who know nothing about sex have been seduced by a culture that is constantly telling them that being sexy gives them power. Giving children attention for their "sexiness" at age six can have heartbreaking consequences at twelve.

The PBS documentary "The Lost Children of Rockdale County"[12] reports on an outbreak of syphilis among twelve- to fourteen-year-olds in a wealthy suburb of Atlanta in 1994. More than two hundred children were infected. There is a poignant scene in which the interviewer asks three thirteen-year-old girls about their sexual activity. One of them picks up a bunch of Beanie Babies and starts showing the interviewer how to have group sex. It is heartbreaking—not just because of the behavior—but because of the sad and vacuous expressions that emerge on their faces between the nervous giggles and bravado.

Rockdale County is not unique. The factors that led to the outbreak of syphilis are common to most American communities:

1. A culture saturated in sexually provocative stimulation aimed at children.
2. Parents who work and mistakenly assume that because their children are older they can be left alone between 3:00 p.m. to 6:00 p.m.
3. Teens with unstructured and unsupervised time and easy access to X-rated DVDs or cable TV and alcohol.

We can all learn something from those young girls in Rockdale County. We can start by not fooling ourselves into thinking that our kids have not been exposed to this kind of activity, and understanding how it is affecting their behavior.

The Sexualized Child

Although we don't often discuss it, the value of sexy is a given in our culture. Sexy is powerful. Sexy is exciting. Sexy sells. Drop into any playground or walk with the students as they change classes in middle school and you witness firsthand how completely our children have incorporated the value of sexy. If you still have doubts, try buying not-sexy clothes for your daughter (regardless of her age). Raised in an environment where power and social prestige is equated with looking and acting sexy, many children have incorporated the power aspects of sex into their self-image long before their bodies have felt the first hormonal twinges of sexual desire.

Alisa, an eleven-year-old, enters my office with all the bored facade of a sixteen-year-old, her prepubescent body at odds with the low-slung jeans, belly shirt, highlighted hair, and full mani/pedicure. She flops onto the couch with as much annoyance as she can muster and tells me how ridiculous it is that her parents want her to come to therapy simply because her grades haven't been "as perfect as they want them to be." In fact, Alisa has entered middle school with a vengeance. When Alisa was invited to parties by the popular older kids, her parents were initially pleased with her newfound popularity but now describe her as "obsessed" with her social life. "It's like she can't unplug, ever," says her mom, who has failed at limiting Alisa's Internet and social time. Always an A student, she has now become disinterested in schoolwork, music lessons, and Girl Scouts—all the activities that had been important to her in elementary school. A couple of months into therapy, Alisa tells me about a party for an out-of-town friend, where she "hooked up" with an older boy in the bathroom.

"He wanted me to give him, you know, a hand job. So, like, I was doing it and everything and when he got to that point, you know, right before he does it, then I stopped and laughed at him and ran out of the room."

She relates this story with a conspiratorial glee, as if she were telling me that she had managed to trick her parents into letting her stay up past midnight.

"Was this fun?" I ask.

"No, not really," she answers, "After I started I wasn't sure I wanted to. It kind of grossed me out."

"Why would you do something that grossed you out?" I ask.

"I don't know, I just thought it'd be a good story to tell my friends."

Taking on the persona of a fully sexual adult before their bodies have experienced any adult feelings of sexual desire can have far-reaching consequences. It's a frightening thing to see a child who has become sexualized before his or her time, playing with a power they cannot possibly fathom. Alisa is not unique. A great many children have come to believe that their social success depends on acquiring the power of sex before they have experienced their own sexuality or even understood what sex really is.

In 2007, the American Psychological Association (APA) linked eating disorders, low self-esteem, and depression with the early sexualization of girls. Although the effect of sexualization on boys was not studied, several components of sexualization—as defined by the APA—could equally be applied to the way our culture "inappropriately imposes sexuality" on our sons.[13] What's happening to our daughters, teaching them to "work" their sexy as a way to attain social power before they've grown into their sexuality, is relatively new and is justifiably causing alarm. But our sons are being sexualized as well, with video games like Duke Nukem, reality TV, and popular music. However, this seems to be causing less of a stir, perhaps because teaching little boys that sex is an entitlement that is often linked to violence is not really new.

Culturally, we have always understood that sex can be used or bartered for power and prestige: men who establish their power through sexual "conquest," the struggling actress who gives sexual favor for a shot at stardom. With reality TV shows like *Survivor* and *The Appentice*, this aggressive use of sexuality to gain power is now collectively applauded. We watch with amusement as men and women use their sexuality to lie and manipulate each other in order to win large sums of money. But when our eleven- and twelve-year-olds, particularly our daughters, begin to aggressively use sex for social status, we are appalled. Given the 44.5 hours of media (TV, movies, music, video games, and the Internet) that American children (eight to eighteen) consume every week,[14] should we be surprised that sex has become a benefit to be bought and sold?

Removing Sex From Intimacy

Another striking difference in how our children have come to understand sex is the fashionable trend to separate having sex from any need for intimacy or relationship. The expression "hooking up" doesn't so much describe a specific sexual behavior (it can be used to mean anything from kissing to intercourse) as it signifies a detached attitude toward the person one is hooking up with. The act of being intimate is relegated to a convenient pastime.

Janet, a sixteen-year-old, is in therapy because she is cutting herself.

"Hooking up is just what you do. You go to a party and people hook up. No one wants to go out with someone, that's way too complicated."

"You mean it's too complicated to be seeing just one person."

"Yeah, it's just that if you do that, you're letting the person know you like them, then it's really easy to get hurt. Maybe they don't like you. When you hook up, it's just for fun, and if the other person doesn't like you, it's OK because you were just hooking up, it's just hormones."

Knowing how hurt Janet feels most of the time, I add, "It seems like people can get hurt anyway."

"Yeah, but when you call it hooking up, nobody knows."

Hooking up satisfies the hormones without having to engage in all that messy stuff involved in relationship. If you hook up, you have distanced yourself from having to look like you care about whether or not the person you hooked up with cares about you. In a time of instant messaging, it's so much more economical than having to figure out how you feel.

In an interview with a *New York Times* reporter, Brian, a sixteen-year-old, put it this way: "Being in a real relationship just complicates everything. You feel obligated to be all, like, couple-ly. And that gets really boring after a while. When you're friends with benefits, you go over, hook up, then play video games or something."[15]

The teen expression "friend with benefits" ("fwb" in instant-messaging lingo) captures this sex-as-commodity attitude. A friend with benefits is a person you have sex with, with no strings attached, no intimacy is required, i.e., a preestablished hookup partner. Sex is the benefit.[16]

James, at seventeen, has come into therapy with what he calls an addiction to recreational drugs that he has no intention of giving up. Functioning adequately in school, he feels justified in medicating away what he calls "the ridiculous pointlessness of living." James has had a friend with benefits since sophomore year, a girl, he says, that he's "addicted to fucking." I ask if the relationship is satisfying.

"Well, I mean I get off, if that's what you mean, but I have to be totally wiped to do it with her."

"What about her?"

"You mean, does she like it? I don't know, we never talk."

There was a time when having sex without intimacy was considered a clinical disorder. Now it's an accepted practice on college campuses, high schools,[17] and middle schools and common fare on network programming for teens. On college campuses, a "booty call," or request for sexual favors, can be made via the Internet, turning sex into a commodity to be consumed and forgotten like take-out food. Considering the number of adolescents and young adults cutting themselves, taking antidepressants, and self-medicating with illegal drugs, I can't help but wonder if this fashionable disconnect of physical intimacy from emotional connection, of viewing sex as a commodity to be acquired and discarded, is not linked to the pain some teens struggle to control.[18]

Why Kids Are So Confused

It's no wonder that teens have embraced the power of sexy, and separated sexual pleasure from emotional intimacy. They are simply reflecting a culture that has dissected the amazing complexity of human sexuality into separate industries, using each aspect of sex as a marketing strategy. Kids don't understand how sex, as in the biology of reproduction, relates to the attention they get from looking sexy. How do those gushy feelings of desire that they get when "he/she looks at me that way" have to do with love? And how in the world are teens supposed to sort out how physical they want to get with someone? Are there rules? Is it all about feeling good, or is there something more involved? Each aspect of sexuality seems to exist in a universe unto itself. To make matters even more difficult, kids tend to learn about these different aspects of sex from entirely different sources. And no one is connecting the dots.

There is the *biology* aspect of sex that involves reproduction. Biology sex belongs to science, sex-ed classes, and the Discovery Channel. Most often, it's the only aspect of sexuality that a child ever hears an adult talk to them about. From a kid's point of view, biology sex is embarrassing, technical, kind of gross, and somehow related to babies and disease.

Then there is the *social power* aspect of sex, the sex of being sexy and popular used by advertisers to sell us everything from toothpaste to lingerie. The social power of sex is very important to preteens and teens as they define their social/sexual identity and try to establish their place in the social hierarchy of their peers. Using the power of sex as a tool to get what you want is explicitly taught by the media and is reinforced by peers. The explosion in emphasis of the social power aspect of sex is altering how our kids define their sexuality.

The *sexual desire* aspect of sex is a physical feeling that teens experience inside themselves. These new feelings of sexual desire can overwhelm teens and interfere with their ability to make healthy decisions. More often than not, no one is helping kids make sense out of the power of sexual desire or teaching them about the inner strength people need to bring desire under their control.

The *relationship* aspect of sex involves intimacy, love, romance, music, poetry, and varying levels of commitment. Kids learn about relationships and commitment from watching the people around them as well as from media and the arts. Few teens have conversations with caring adults about what constitutes a healthy, loving relationship. Many kids tell us that sex is OK if you're in love. But what does this mean? We rarely ask them what love means to them or help them think through how they would know if they love someone, or if someone loves them.

And finally there is the *moral/ethical* aspect of sex. What is the right thing to do? What principles of human behavior do you apply to deciding when, how, and with whom to have sex? Historically this is where religion weighs in, offering a way of understanding the role of sex in our lives and setting guidelines for sexual behavior. Some parents align with their religious guidelines and are looking for ways of making these guidelines relevant to their children in a culture that does not support those values. Some parents align with some aspects of their religion's sexual guidelines but not others and are sorting through what they want to say to their children. Some parents are looking for a way to discuss ethical sexual behavior without using religious guidelines. Most of us could use a road map for thinking through what our values are and how we can make them relevant to our child's experience, not just at twelve but throughout their life.

The challenge of this book is to pull all of these different aspects of sex together; to connect the dots between the *biology of sex, sexual power, sexual desire, sexual intimacy*, and *sexual ethics*, to offer a way of sorting through our values concerning sex so we can find the words to convey our values to our children.

take it home

1. As you go through your day, be aware how often your children are exposed to sexual messages on the radio, TV, video games, billboards, in magazines, etc. What assumptions are they making about the world?
2. Do you have religious guidelines that you wish to convey to your teens with regard to sexual behavior?
3. What do your kids know about the power of looking sexy? Do you think it's important to discuss how to use that power?
4. Do they understand what sexual desire is?
5. What have you told your children about love? Do they know the difference between having loving feelings for someone and having lustful feelings for them? What does love have to do with sex?
6. How would you define responsible sexual behavior?

• • • • • • • • • • • • • • •

two

Healthy Sexual Attitudes
Start with Respect

L earning to be a healthy and responsible sexual person starts at birth. "Sex education" begins when we validate an infant's right to listen to the needs of his or her own body. We do this by articulating and responding appropriately to both their desire to be touched and need to be left alone.

Toddlers will raise their arms to us, asking to be picked up. We teach them how to ask for what they want when we match their request with the appropriate words: "Do you want to come up?" As we lift them into our arms, we have validated their need for connection with both our words and actions.

If you watch carefully, you will see that even the youngest baby can signal when they need to be left alone. By repeatedly turning their head away from an exuberant older sibling or well-meaning aunt, they let us know they've had enough stimulation. Again we articulate their need, "You don't want to play now, we can play later," and help them establish the space they need by removing them from the stimulation.

As they get older this can sometimes mean that Grammy or Aunt Margie or even we don't get all the physical contact we might want. By two years old, children will often assert their newfound autonomy by aggressively rejecting our desire for a hug. As painful as this might be for us, how wonderful that they are learning that it is their right to say yes or no to physical intimacy. ("You don't want a hug right now. I can wait and hug you when you want a hug.") What better way to teach them that touching must be by mutual consent than by respecting their wishes?

Forcing children to hug and kiss people they don't know or do not feel close to disrespects their personal integrity and initiates a pattern of understanding intimacy as a form of obligation. It is particularly unpleasant to see a child forced to hug an adult and then rewarded with a gift. What exactly are we teaching them with that behavior?

Setting Boundaries for Sexual Behavior

All of us are sexual beings from the moment we're conceived. Although our adult sexuality does not ignite until puberty, touching or rubbing our genitals as a form of stimulation and relaxation can begin while we are still in the womb. We continue our child's "sex education" by consistently validating and articulating their feelings. At the same time, like so many other aspects of parenting, we set boundaries for their behavior that are in alignment with our family values.

We understand that our four-year-old may rub her clitoris as a way of comforting herself, and at the same time we teach her the boundaries that we place around that behavior. We don't humiliate or embarrass her, but we do teach her how to restrict that behavior so that she is not vulnerable to the attention or ridicule of others. As members of a culture and perhaps a religion that places restrictions on when, where, or even if masturbation is allowed, we let our children know, at an early age, that although touching their genitals feels nice, this is an activity that takes place in private. Beginning the conversation about sexy feelings at an early age, we become the primary source of information and guidance at a time when our opinion is still more important than their peers'. Creating a foundation for healthy sexual development as well as respectful intimacy involves:

1. Responding when they want to be touched and respecting their desire to be left alone.
2. Never pressuring or rewarding a child for being physically intimate.
3. Acknowledging the pleasure that comes from masturbation and putting boundaries around where and when such behavior can take place, in alignment with cultural norms and/or your family's personal or religious convictions.

Sex and Santa—Innocence Is Not the Same as Ignorance

Despite my best parenting efforts, my son at age seven already had a connection in his mind linking sex and violence. Captive on the playground, it had been exciting to listen while his second-grade peers talked about a video game in which naked women were a reward for killing people. His first exposure to sexual images had not been in my control. This was a wake-up call. It was clear that no matter how vigilant I was about his access to television, films, radio, and video games, I would not be able to control how or when he and his older sister (age nine) were going to hear about sex. Parenting had taken on a new dimension. As a mother, I intended to raise a healthy, responsible human being yet I couldn't even prevent his first introduction to sexuality being in the context of degradation and violence. What chance did I have of giving him a foundation for understanding sexuality that was based on beauty and wonder? How was I going to raise a healthy, responsible man?

Well, if I couldn't prevent, I could proactively educate. I was determined that when it came to finding out how babies were made, I was going to get there first. It was time for "the talk."

Most kids in America today learn something about the mechanics of sexual intercourse by the time they are eight years old, usually on the school bus or playground. What had my nine-year-old daughter already been exposed to? Being proactive, educating, and giving my kids a context through which they can assess all the things they will see and hear was really my only choice. Yes, ages seven and nine seemed ridiculously young to be telling them about sexual intercourse, but if they were going to be hearing stuff, let them know the truth in a context of wonder and appreciation, and let them hear it from me. Oh, and, by the way, they both still believed in Santa Claus. That's the world we live in.

What's the connection between Santa Claus and sex? It has something to do with how we as parents need to maintain an image of our children as being innocent and pure. The Santa Claus/sex connection comes up frequently in my public lectures to parents. Often a mother will ask, incredulously, if she really needs to tell her nine-year-old about sex. After all, "She's so innocent; she still believes in Santa Claus." It seems that in our culture, not believing in Santa and knowing the real deal about how babies are made somehow symbolizes the end of innocence. It's time to rethink this. If our children lived on a farm, the facts of reproduction would be as ordinary and innocent as having breakfast. Learning the mechanics of sexual intercourse—in a context of love and respect—does not take away the innocence or purity from our children. Perhaps it feels that way because we remember the less-than-inspiring way we first heard about sex. But we can do better. Think about what purity and innocence really mean. Allowing our sons to learn about sex in the context of violence and humiliation, because we're too embarrassed to talk with them, destroys their innocence. Dressing our daughters up at four and five years old in over-the-top, sexy "costumes" and teaching them to wriggle provocatively for a "dance" recital destroys their innocence.[1] But telling our children about the biology of their own creation, in a manner that respects the wonder of life, love, and intimacy, is a gift we need to give.

Explaining the Biology of Sex: Of Course You Feel Weird; Do It Anyway

I wish I could say that telling my kids about the biology of reproduction was easy. After all, I am a psychologist who specializes in teen sexual behavior. But I'd be lying. The whole thing seemed really weird.

When I was ten years old, I asked my mother what sex was. I remember that she looked horrified and asked in a "How could you be so stupid?" tone of voice, "Haven't you seen dogs do it?"

"Do what?" I asked.

"You know . . . climb on top of each other," she responded, clearly perturbed at needing to elaborate.

The conversation didn't get much better. Years later, she told me that her introduction to the mechanics of sexual intercourse was from the boy down the street who told her that babies come because "boys peed inside girls." We all carry a lot of baggage when it comes to sex, but in the culture that we are living in today, the stakes are too high to let our baggage get in the way.

Hoping to do better, I purchased a wonderful little book called *Where Did I Come From?*[2] It was full of plump, naked little hand-drawn figures of "mommies and daddies" who "feel very loving" toward each other. Sexual excitement, culminating in intercourse, is explained in words that respect a child's perspective. After looking at several books, I picked this one because it was consistent with my values. My criteria were:

- age-appropriate level of the language
- a positive, loving context for sexuality
- a sense of wonder, enthusiasm, humor, and an overall lightness

I read it first, a couple of times, imagining all the questions my kids might have. I discussed it at length with their father and together we told the kids we had something important to talk with them about. We told them they were old enough to hear about how it is that people create more people, how babies are made. We told them that they might start to hear things about this thing called sex from their friends in school, but that in our family we considered this something private. We let them know that if they had questions about anything they heard about sex, they could come to their dad or me. We also let them know that it was not their job to educate their friends, and that different parents have different ideas about sex and what they want their kids to know.

Because this is a private thing, they should keep this information to themselves. Here again, we are reinforcing that when it comes to sex there are boundaries we place around behavior and we expect them to respect those boundaries.

We sat on the floor in my bedroom, our backs against the bed, my daughter curled up next to me. My son, however, announced that he did not need to read this book and plopped onto the bed behind us, pulling the covers over his head.

There was a time when professionals, like myself, told parents to "let the child guide you" with regard to telling kids about sex. Parents were instructed to wait until the child came to them with questions and then to answer according to the child's age. This is good advice, to a point. Every child is different and some kids simply never ask. This does not mean, however, that they have not been gathering a great deal of information about sex that they're struggling to understand.

We need to get to our children first and establish ourselves as the source of information. Some kids will ask and how you respond is everything. Give it some thought right now. Talk to your partner or friends. If you seem embarrassed, too busy, put off by your children's questions, or if you give vague or silly answers, they will not see you as a source of information and they will go elsewhere. That said, a three-year-old who asks, "How did the baby get into your belly?" does not need lengthy discussion about sperm and eggs. The same question from a mature six-year-old could be answered more explicitly. Certainly by the time the child is eight, start thinking about initiating the conversation. Unless you're living in a cave, by age eight your child has already heard something about sex. *Bottom line: know your kid, don't put it off, think it through first with a partner or friend, and start talking.*

• •

take it home

1. What does your child know about sex? If he had questions, would he come to you?
2. Who do you know that can help you do a practice run-through before you talk to your child about sex?
3. What resources, books, friends, relatives, tapes are available to you?
4. What's standing in the way of having this conversation today? When will you have it?

• •

My son's embarrassment, hiding under the covers behind me, was curious. It was out of character for him not to want to see everything his big sister was seeing. I knew that to take this response as an indication he was too young would be a mistake. My sense was he had been embarrassed by the "hooker and stripper" game, and was feeling funny about returning to an embarrassing subject. This "talk" was happening just in time to keep me in the loop.

"I'm not reading this," he announced again as he secured the blanket over his eyes. "That's OK," I replied. "I think this is really interesting stuff, but you don't have to read it. Just stay here and keep us company." He never said another word, but every time I turned a page I could see him peeking out from under the blanket, completely enthralled.

At the end, my daughter asked the same question I remember

asking my mother when I finally figured out what she was talking about.

"You mean that you and Daddy had to do that every time you wanted to have a baby?" My daughter added, "That is soooo gross!"

You've got to admit, from the perspective of one who has not yet experienced sexual desire, sexual intercourse sounds pretty gross. After all, the parts of the body that we use to reproduce are the same parts a child associates with peeing and pooping.

"Before my body changed into a grown-up body, I thought sex sounded pretty gross, too," I replied. "What's amazing is that after your body changes, you don't feel that way anymore. When your body becomes a grown-up body, you actually think all this stuff sounds pretty cool."

When it comes to explaining the biological aspect of sex, there are a few points you want to make sure you include:

1. Sex is a wonderful thing that grown-ups do when they love and care for each other. Children do not have grown-up bodies, so they are not ready to have sex.
2. They can count on you to make sure that when the time comes for their body to change into a grown-up body, you will give them the information they need to be prepared.
3. You are the primary source of information about sex, and you are willing and happy to answer all questions.
4. Sex is a private thing, and each family has their own way of talking about it. They should not share information that you have given them with others.

Biology Book Sex: It's Only the Beginning

My response to the "hookers and strippers" incident was to proactively educate my son about the facts of sexual intercourse in a
way that respected my values. Duke Nukem woke me up to the
reality that if I was going to raise sexually healthy adults I had to
start the process much earlier than I had imagined. But I had only
addressed the biology aspect of sex. I had given my kids the sit-
on-the-edge-of-the-bed, book-in-hand "talk." There was a great
deal of information still missing.

By fifth or sixth grade most kids in America will get a more
advanced version of biology book sex in sex ed class, an often
overwhelming hodgepodge of anatomical facts involving words
like "sperm," "eggs," "vaginas," and "testicles," assorted diagrams,
and, perhaps, some reassuring and hygienic words about menstruation. We stuff a lot of information in the box called "biology book sex." Because this is the place where we explain how
babies are made, we often add a bunch of scary statistics about
unwanted pregnancy. With the advent of AIDS, we've expanded
the box to include the terrifying realities of HIV and other sexually transmitted diseases (STDs). This way of talking about sex
can be so scary that ten- and eleven-year-olds have actually asked
me if there are any other ways people can have babies. They've
decided that whatever sex is, it simply sounds much too risky.
But fast-forward three or four years, add the biological realities of
sexual desire and adolescent feelings of omnipotence, and kids are
no longer so afraid. What's left is the feeling that the adults have
lied to them. And we have. We have lied by omission.

take it home

1. Do you remember when you first learned about sexual intercourse? Who told you? What did you think about it? What questions did you have? Who could you go to for answers?

2. If you have already discussed biology sex with your child, how have you connected it to the idea of being sexy?

3. If your child has questions, will he or she come to you?

three

·················

Wanting to Be Sexy
Before Their Time

telling my son how babies are made in no way helped him make sense out of the excitement that he had shared with the boys in the playground. What was the connection between naked ladies in a video game and the reproduction stuff of sperm, eggs, and babies? I had to go further. I had to give him a context, a way of thinking about the cultural aspects of sex. I needed to give him some perspective that would help him make sense out of why everything sexy seemed to hold such importance, so that he would have a way to process and assess all the things I could not prevent him from being exposed to.

The vital piece missing from biology-book-sex, from sex ed curriculums, and from how we talk to our kids about sex, is the fuel that keeps the whole process running, sexual desire and its complement, the power that comes from being sexy. The human species continues because as adults, each of us has the power to activate sexual desire and to have our sexual desire activated. If we stop and think about it, the importance we give to being sexy comes from the fact that being sexy gives one the power to stimulate sexual desire. What else is sexy for?

But we never talk to our kids about it. We teach them about reproduction, but we leave out the force, the power that drives us to reproduce. We imagine they're too young to talk about sexual desire because they haven't experienced it yet. In a different place and time that might be true, but in our culture kids are being sold the value and power of sexy from the moment they see the first magazine cover or toothpaste ad with no framework for understanding what they're being sold.

The power of sexy is everywhere—on billboards as we're driving our kids to school, checkout lines in the supermarket, in song lyrics, and advertisements on the radio. Sex is the currency of success for television shows and is inescapable on the Internet. Yet somehow we never imagine that our kids are seeing it or ingesting the value our culture places on being sexy. We never stop and ask how our children are understanding all of this stuff. How is he or she making sense of it? What is it telling them about how to get attention? How will all of this affect how they see themselves or the decisions they make as they develop an adult sexual body? Selling the power of sexy is as pervasive as the air we breathe in America and, like the air, we only really focus on it when it becomes so polluted we're choking. News of teens having oral sex on a school bus[1] offends our sensibilities and gets our attention, at least long enough for a two-minute piece on CNN.

A few years ago, I pitched a story idea about teaching kids how to control and direct the power of their sexual desire to a national columnist, for her parenting column. "Desire is the elephant in the room that we cannot discuss with kids," she replied. "No one wants to talk with kids about sexual desire."

How in the world are kids supposed to learn how to become

responsible sexual people if we don't help them understand that being sexy is powerful because it activates desire and that this desire is hardwired into all living creatures as a way of continuing the species through procreation?

We live in a strange culture in which we have no problem surrounding our children with sexually explicit images, songs, games, humor, and even go so far as to dress them in sexually provocative clothes. Yet we agonize over how to initiate a conversation about sexual desire. It's time to get over it. The whole topic of sex, from Victoria's Secret ads and "how babies are made," to sexual abuse and MTV, none of it makes any sense if you don't understand the role of desire.

What's Going On in Middle School?

What happens when kids have fully ingested the value and power of being sexy before they've ever experienced sexual desire? When little girls practice "shaking their booty" and beg for shorts with "Juicy" written across the butt[2] before they even know why shaking their butt elicits attention? When little boys begin to develop a sexual identity that links sex with power and violence long before experiencing their first spontaneous erection? Initiated into the power of sexy long before their hormones deliver the physical sensation of sexual desire, what happens when the hormones *do* kick in?

Middle School

There has been a lot written in recent years about the complexities of educating the middle school student, that unformed gosling of a creature not yet even a full-blown teen but no longer a child.[3] One factor that contributes to the intensity of this age that I have witnessed over and over again in my private practice is the anxiety and pressure middle school students feel about having to deliver on this thing they've been playing at called sexuality.

The questions most frequently asked by fifth graders when I teach my sexual health curriculum are, "What are the bases? When are you supposed to do the bases? And how will I know what to do?" These children are ten years old. Ninety-nine percent of them have not experienced even an inkling of sexual desire yet they are anxious to grasp the sexual expectations that they know will greet them in middle school. Initiated into the attention-getting power of being sexy, long before they've experienced sexual desire, they enter the halls of middle school feeling like they have to hit the road running.

Preteens, sexualized by a culture that has sold them the power of sex in childhood, enter middle school preprogrammed to act out on their first feelings of sexual desire. Added to the mix is a media actively targeting this age group, eager to capitalize on their physical awkwardness and sexual curiosity, and a new, unsupervised way of exploring their social/sexual identity, the Internet (see Chapter 10). The power of sexy collides with the new feeling of sexual desire in a sexually saturated environment that often offers little adult supervision, a perfect storm.

What does any of this have to do with the kind of sex they've been learning about in health class? What does the being "sexy" sex of MTV and "the new CW"[4] have to do with the biology sex of sexual reproduction? In kids' minds, absolutely nothing. This is the sex of being sexy, of "hooking up," "going the bases," "being in play"—the sex of having the power to use those first signs of a sexual body to excite sexual desire. In kids' minds, the sex of sexual desire is in a universe altogether separate from sexual reproduction.

What kids want us to help them understand is how to handle the feelings that come with sexual desire and how to responsibly use the power that comes from looking or acting sexy. Reproduction is decades away, another lifetime, when you're thirteen. They're trying to make sense out of the power they've begun to experience when people look at them "that way," the excitement their bodies are beginning to experience, and why everyone is so into it on TV. They want to make sense out of the sex of sexual stimulation and desire. What does it mean, and how are they supposed to know what to do with it?

But when it comes to this kind of sex, we are silent. In our anxiety and fear, we have made our presentation of sex so scientific that it is just a set of big words, scary statistics, and "gross" facts about human anatomy. It has no meaning in the day-to-day lives of teens, no value, no connection to their experience of their bodies, and no relationship to the world they're living in. By omitting sexual desire from our conversations about sex, we lose our credibility and leave them ill-prepared to cope with inner feelings or outer pressures. When we don't get there first and give kids a way of understanding the hypersexualized culture that they're in, when we don't know that the TV in their bedroom is like an abusive parent—socializing them to connect sex with power and not intimacy—our kids begin to play at being sexy, in dangerous ways, before they've ever had a sexual feeling. A sexually provocative environment, without adult guidance to help make sense of it, is overwhelming and emotionally dangerous.

Helping kids understand the relationship between reproduction and desire in no way implies that sexual desire should only be used for the purpose of reproduction. When and under what circumstances someone should have sex is a critical part of this conversation that we will explore fully in Chapter 8 on ethics and religion.

Why Start This Conversation Early?

It may seem unsettling to talk with our children about sexual desire before they have experienced it, but there are vital reasons to give them a framework for understanding desire before they've had sexual feelings:

1. By the time they begin to have sexual feelings of their own, they are much more resistant to listening to anything you have to say on the subject.
2. You can give them an ethical framework that becomes the filter through which they interpret the cultural messages about sexual desire and sexual power.
3. You establish yourself as a valuable resource.
4. Your involvement as parent serves to defuse the high intensity peer-and-media-manipulated titillation that can be overwhelming for a preteen.

We start talking *before* they inherit their full-blown sexual desire. We give them a way of thinking about desire and power before they have actually experienced it. This way, as they begin to try and make sense of the sexual environment we live in, they will carry with them our framework for understanding sex—a perspective that is not based on titillation and consumerism—but on wonder, responsibility, and love.

take it home

1. What does your child understand about the power of being sexy?
2. What forms of media is your child exposed to that would reinforce sexy as a way of getting power and attention?
3. Do family, friends, or peers reinforce sexy as a way of getting attention?

four

....

Starting the Conversation About Desire and the Power of Sexy

as a species, we're hardwired to survive.

So how do we talk about sex in a way that connects wanting to be sexy, feelings of sexual desire, and human reproduction?

Start simple. Why does it make sense for human beings to have sexual desire? If it makes sense to us, it will make sense to our kids.

Sexual desire is a huge source of power, an amazing energy generator that propels the human race toward reproduction and the continuation of the species. No sex, no human race. Kids are amazed by this fact. Most twelve- and even thirteen-year-olds have never really put together that sex is a necessary part of the continuation of life. It's a good place to start.

•••

Sexual Desire Is Activated ➜ Sex ➜ Reproduction ➜ Survival of the Species

•••

It is this power that continuously pushes the human race to continue making babies. Each of us is hardwired to experience sexual desire, to become owners of this sexual energy at that time in our lives when we become capable of reproduction. We experience feelings of sexual desire when our senses respond to something or someone who is sexy. The flip side of feeling sexual desire is wanting to be the one who activates someone else's desire.

The energy of sexual desire is the fuel that propels us to leave home, find a partner, and begin our own families. It is no accident that we begin to experience sexual desire at that time in our life when we are changing from being a child into an adult. It is this energy that makes us start wanting to be with our friends more than we want to be with our family, that makes our parents look so annoying, and that eventually brings us to a point where we are ready to leave home and learn what we need to know to eventually support a family of our own.

Developing a Healthy Relationship with Our Desires Creates the Foundation for Understanding Sexuality

Even though children have not experienced sexual desire, they have certainly experienced desire. By teaching them how to have a healthy relationship with all of their desires we can prepare them for the overwhelming feelings of sexual desire that arise in adolescence. If we can help our children learn how to identify their desires, to understand how to have desires without being ruled by them, then as they come into their sexuality they are prepared to make healthy sexual choices.

It's not just sexual desire that keeps the human species going.

Many desires act as a fuel to keep our species alive and thriving, like the desire to eat or the desire to protect ourselves. Desires give us the energy to seek out those things we need to survive.

It goes something like this. . . . We are all hardwired to survive. Our senses, our ability to see, hear, touch, and smell, are designed to search out those things we need to survive and send signals to our brain saying, "I need that! I really, really want that!" We can actually feel that energy stirring in our bodies. The energy to have

• •

desire gives us energy

We Are Hardwired to Survive

Our Senses Are Designed to Find Those Things
That Help Us Survive

When Our Senses Locate Something
Connected to Survival, Our Desire Is Activated,
Filling Us with a Huge Energy

We Look for Ways to Release This Energy,
to Fulfill Our Desire

Releasing This Energy Feels Good

So We Do It Again

If We Do It Enough, It Becomes a Habit

• •

the object of our desire builds up inside and moves us to take action and get what we want.

When we finally get the object of our desire, the energy is released and our senses tell us, "Umm, that felt good." We're pretty smart creatures. We remember what feels good and start figuring out ways to do it again. If we do it enough times, a habit is formed (see Chapter 7).

It makes sense that fulfilling our desires feels good; that's why we keep working to satisfy them. Some desires, like the desire for food, we are born with; others, like sexual desire, only happen when our bodies are ready to reproduce. Even very young children can begin to understand that growing up means learning how to control and direct the energy of their desires.

Take Food, for Example

Clearly, we need food to survive. As we get more and more hungry, the desire to eat becomes more and more intense. The energy to get food begins to build inside of us. That energy can propel us to grab a gun and hunt down a tasty morsel for dinner, or it can propel us off the couch to go throw some instant soup in the microwave. Either way, our energy is focused on finding a release. The feeling that we get when we take that first mouthful, when the energy of our desire is released, is very, very pleasurable. We remember that feeling of pleasure and want to do it again and again.

Our senses are the key to this whole process. They are always activating our desires. Just smelling, seeing, or thinking about food can ignite our desire, even if we're not really hungry. What we see, smell, and hear can initiate a chain of physical reactions that energizes us to act. Our bodies are brilliant in responding with desire to any stimulus that is core to our survival. The tricky part is that satisfying our desires feels so good that we will continue to do so even when we no longer need to in order to survive, creating habits of behavior that are hard to break.

Becoming a responsible human being means learning to be the master of our desires. We don't have to feel guilty about our desires; they are a necessary part of our survival. We don't have to be embarrassed or scared of the powerful feelings. We need to know that it is our job to be the one who controls and directs that power so that we, and not our desires, are in control of our lives.

In many ways, food is a great analogy for sex. But unlike the energy we direct toward finding food, which begins the day we are born, the energy for wanting sex does not turn on until we start becoming adults. Having a desire for sex before we're able to care for babies wouldn't make any sense; it would not help us survive as a species. Although we are sexual beings from birth, we do not inherit the sexual power that propels us toward independence and procreation until our bodies change from child to adult. Then we enter a new world where what we see, smell, or hear can ignite a desire for sexual release that is a built-in guarantee that our species will continue. Like food, sex brings us tremendous pleasure. And like food, if we have not learned discrimination and self-discipline, if we have not learned to be the master of that energy, we will be dragged around by our sexual desires, making decisions that can hurt others and ourselves.

When we talk about desire as a form of energy, we open the door to a rich conversation about how this energy is activated, how it can be manipulated, and how we, as human beings, develop the muscle to control this energy. By giving our kids a way of understanding their relationship to all desire, we take sexual desire out of the domain of music videos, defuse the titillation, and show our kids that sex is just another, very important form of energy that we are responsible for learning how to control and direct.

Anger: Another Form of Power and Energy

It pays to have a menu of ways to talk about desire with our kids. What works perfectly for one kid falls flat with another.

Anger is another source of energy that can help us find the language to talk to our kids about desire. As parents, we understand how important it is to talk to our kids about controlling their anger. We understand that the surge of energy we feel that prompts us to strike out when someone hurts us is important and necessary if we have to defend ourselves. From an early age, we teach children appropriate ways to harness this energy. We don't tell them that anger is bad. We teach them how to identify, control, and direct the surge of angry energy. We tell them to use their words. We send them to karate lessons and competitive sports. We teach them the difference between using the energy of anger to defend themselves and using it to bully others. When our kids come home from school full of stories about how someone got into trouble for fighting, or not being able to be quiet in class, they provide us with an opportunity to reinforce the value of learning to control and direct one's energy.

Life is full of occasions where we can choose to control and direct the energy of our desires or suffer the consequence of being dragged around by them. There is nothing more frightening than sitting across from a sixteen-year-old in my office who thinks it is his God-given right to get every desire met, who has never developed the muscle of self-discipline (see Chapter 5), and who is experiencing the intensity of sexual desire. By acknowledging our children's desire at an early age—and by helping them grow the muscle to control their desires—we prepare them for the overwhelming, hormone-driven waves of adolescence. Talking to our children about how our desires create energy—whether it's the desire to eat, the desire to respond to aggression, or the desire to have sex—we help them understand the power of desire, and we make them aware of how their desire is continuously being manipulated by what they see, hear, and smell.

• •

take it home

1. Think of a time when typically your child has a big desire for something. How can you validate that desire and help him or her become aware of how much energy the desire gives him or her? Have him or her rate his or her energy on a scale from one to ten.
2. Think of examples of people who have not learned how to control their energy. Ask your child if he or she can give you some examples.

• •

When People Don't Learn to Control Their Desires

One of the most frequently asked questions I hear from parents is, "How can I talk to my children about sexual abuse?" Protecting our children from abuse involves:

- Proactively teaching them that the sexual parts of their body are private and should never be touched by anyone else with the exception of a doctor.
- Teaching them what they should do if anyone does touch them inappropriately. (Say no in a loud voice and go and tell an adult.)

Most often the parents I'm speaking with have already educated their children about how to protect themselves. What they are asking for is a way of explaining to kids how it is that someone would ever do something like that. They're looking for a way to help children make sense out of an abnormal act without terrifying them. I have found that if we have laid the groundwork by helping kids understand that desires, all kinds of desires, are forms of energy that we must learn how to control, the conversation about sexual abuse is much easier. Although not by any means sufficient for discussing abuse with an older child (twelve and up), the following script covers the basics.

• •

"There are people in the world who have never learned how to control their energy. Instead of being in control of their desires, their desires control them:

- When they want something, they just steal it.
- When they have angry energy, they break things or hurt people.
- When they have sexual energy, they force it on other people.

- It is never right for a grown-up to want to touch a child in a sexy way.
- It is never OK for someone to force what they want on someone else. People who have never learned to control their desires are dangerous. When we find out that someone is not in control of their desires, we protect ourselves by putting dangerous people in prison, where they can't hurt anyone and where they can learn to be in control of themselves."

• •

Letting Them Know We Understand the Power of Sexy

Evan is a pudgy, baby-faced twelve-year-old, who still plays with Matchbox cars. He has walked in on two kids having oral sex in the bathroom at school and is now sitting in my office with his parents, who have asked me to help him make sense out of what he has seen. As I begin to explain how sex is an energy that can be manipulated by what we see and hear, Evan, who up until then seemed to be struggling to understand, suddenly bursts out, "Oh, yeah! Now I get it. It's like those Victoria Secret ads! They make me really hard!" His poor mom almost fell off the couch.

We don't often stop to see how our children's newly experienced sexual energy is being manipulated by the environment or how our kids are being taught to act sexy as a way of acquiring social power. Understanding our own feelings of sexual desire—and how those feelings can be manipulated by what we see and hear—is only one half of the story. The rest is understanding that when we dress and act in a sexual way, we have the power to manipulate the sexual energy in others, and with that power comes great responsibility.

Every thirteen-year-old girl who walks down the corridors of middle school in a tight-fitting tank top feels the power of being sexy. It's an amazing feeling. But adults never acknowledge that power. We never let them know that we understand how over-the-top exciting it is to shift the energy in a room by how you dress or talk. We don't give them a context to understand how this power can be used or the responsibilities they have, to themselves and one another, when they begin to play with their sexual energy.

Part of the excitement and adventure of being a teen is figuring out who you are as a social/sexual person. Teens have always explored their newfound sexual power, but never in such an intensely saturated sexual environment, with no rules, for such a long period of their lives. Most kids today need to find a way of negotiating the responsibilities that come from having sexual energy for about fifteen to twenty years before they decide to use that energy to create a family of their own. They need a way of thinking about sex that will sustain their health and personal integrity from pre-adolescence, through college and beyond.

We start by not only preparing them for the powerful feelings of sexual desire, but also by letting them know that we understand the amazing experience of having someone look at you in "that way," that we understand the social power that comes from looking and acting sexy. In a culture that is selling children the power of sexy long before they experience sexual desire, we need to help them understand that exploring the power of looking sexy is not for children but reserved for when your body and mind begin transforming into adulthood, and even then there are rules for how to use this power responsibly. When we feel free to discuss with our kids both sexual desire and the excitement that comes from stimulating desire in others, we begin to disengage them from the media myth that sexuality is the sole domain of the young and beautiful and marketers intent on selling grooming products. We make learning about sexuality part of how we engage as a family. We let kids know that figuring out how to use one's sexual energy is complicated and that, even as adults, we continue to learn how to deal with our sexuality with integrity to ourselves and those we love. By acknowledging the intensity and wonder of sexual feelings, we set the stage for discussing how that energy can be expressed, manipulated, abused, and transformed.

Who's Manipulating Your Desire?
Whose Desire Are You Manipulating?

If you want to get a teen's attention, tell him he's being manipulated. An adolescent is just beginning to understand that the world is a complicated game and that he or she doesn't quite know all the rules. They bristle at the thought that people are taking advantage of them. And people are.

Desire, any kind of desire, can be increased or decreased by what we see, hear, taste, feel, and smell or think about. Sexual desire is no different. The same way that a television ad for Sara Lee fresh banana cake can make a guy raid the refrigerator, Victoria's Secret ads can give him a hard-on. In both cases desire has been manipulated for the purpose of selling. And it's not only the media that's doing the manipulating. Just as a sexy picture or song manipulates our sexual desire, we manipulate each other's sexual desire. When I'm talking with teens I will often ask, "If an attractive lady walked into the classroom right now wearing only a skimpy bikini, what would happen to the sexual energy in this room?" They all giggle and point toward the sky. A single person has the power to change the atmosphere of any environment by simply dressing in a way that raises sexual desire. In the same way that the media can manipulate sexual desire, we all manipulate one another's sexual desire. It seems obvious, but how often do we talk about the fact that each of us has the sexual power to change the atmosphere of the environment we're in? How often do we discuss the responsibilities that come with having that power?

Fitting Your Sexy to the Task at Hand

How many of us have gone shopping with our children and been unable to find school clothes or play clothes that don't make us feel uncomfortable because of their obviously provocative design? But what can we do? Everyone seems to be dressing that way. How many of us have sat in a church or synagogue and been distracted by a neighbor who walks in dressed in an overtly sexual manner? Perhaps we have rolled our eyes, dismayed that someone would dress that way in an environment meant for inward focus and sacred prayer.

At a conservative synagogue, the rabbi, who had asked me to join him in creating a class on ethical sexual behavior for bar and bat mitzvah students, asked his congregation to take responsibility for maintaining the sacred intention of the synagogue. He understood that it was pointless to hold the teens in the class to a higher standard than their parents. He wanted to empower the community to take responsibility for upholding the sacred atmosphere of the synagogue by addressing the responsibility that we all have to each other, to dress in a manner that fits the task at hand. This meant to dress in a way that kept the sexual energy reduced enough to honor the intention of communal worship in a holy space. Before starting the teen class, he sent a flyer to the entire congregation titled "*Tz'niut*." Expounding on this beautiful Hebrew word that refers to modesty and human respect, he called on his congregation to exert "strong communal pressure" to assist those who would do more than "bemoan the lack of adherence to Jewish values and concretize the value of *tz'niut* in daily life." This flyer set a standard and started a dialogue that continues today.

"With Great Power Comes Great Responsibility"[1]

As we're discussing sexual power with our teen, it's not enough to simply acknowledge the power; we have to discuss the myriad ways that power can be used and abused. We need to share the subtle discriminations necessary to know when it's OK to look and act sexy, and when it's not OK. How one chooses to dress is not only a matter of freedom to express one's personal style, but it is also an expression of social responsibility to the time, place, people, and activity that one is choosing to engage in.

In my sexual health and responsibility class, we talk about fluctuating hormones and how boys, during this time of extreme hormone surges, can get spontaneous erections. Although erections can happen for no reason at all, they can also be caused by something visually stimulating. I ask the class how many of them think it's easy to learn algebraic formulas while dealing with a spontaneous erection. After the moans and groans and "this is so disgusting" have died down, they get the point. If you're in math class, dress to learn math and understand that inheriting an adult body comes with the responsibility of knowing how to use your sexual power in a responsible way. These conversations can get complicated. Why is it OK to be sexually alluring on the beach? What makes that different? How about at dances? How sexy is too sexy and how sexy is the right amount of sexy? There are no easy answers, and we will never all agree.

What If There Were a "Sexuality Quotient"?

Let's say, for the purpose of discussion, we could create a sexuality quotient that would help us match our level of sexy to the task at hand. On a scale of one to ten, what would the sexuality quotient (SQ) for math class be? Two? Three? More than that would interfere with math, so when considering how to dress for math class, belly shirts and exposed underwear (yes, how boys dress matters, too) don't work because they raise the SQ above a two. On the other hand, most of us understand that the SQ at the beach is acceptable at an eight or nine. Why? Great question, I have no idea. Skimpy bikinis have the power to raise the level of sexual energy to a nine, which for some reason we all agree is perfectly fine for the beach. (Perhaps because all we need to do at the beach is experience the power of each other's sexuality and then run into the water.) We can have fun playing with this idea of a sexuality quotient, but there are serious reasons to help our teens get the point. Kids need to hear from us that there are times and places where dressing at an SQ of an eight or nine is just not safe. Going into the city at night on public transportation means taking your sexy down a notch or two.

Being responsible and safe means figuring out what level of sexy is

- safe
- responsive to the task at hand
- in alignment with your intention.

Sleeping next to someone in your college dorm with only your underwear on when you have no intention of having sex with him or her raises the SQ to a level that is not in alignment with your intention and is not safe. If you're a woman, this lack of awareness can put you at risk for assault or rape. If you are a man, it can put you at risk for not acting according to your values and misunderstanding the desires of the person whom you're with.

It's important to be very clear here. *Being conscious of how your sexuality impacts on the environment is not the same as being the cause of someone else losing control of their sexual energy.* When I'm talking to a group of parents, this is the point where a mother will very rightly ask if I'm not "blaming the girls" for boys acting inappropriately. No. I would love to live in a world where each of us has mastered our sexual desires such that anyone can dress any way they choose and feel safe. But that is not our world. In the meantime, I have to hear the date rape stories of girls who might have been able to avoid tragic consequences if someone had talked to them about the way the world is. Enough. Obviously, the victim is never to blame. As parents, there is no excuse for not teaching our sons and daughters that it is their responsibility to control their sexual desire. As a culture we must hold each individual accountable if they do not. But not to let our daughters know the risk they take when they raise the sexual energy in a given environment is unconscionable.

The sexuality quotient is a tool, a way of acknowledging our teen's newfound sexual power. It gives us a way of making sense of emotionally charged subjects, such as how kids dress, behave at parties and dances, and portray themselves on the Internet. Because we are talking about sex as a powerful energy that we can delight in expressing and at the same time learn to how to control in a socially responsible way, we are in a good position to address the multitude of considerations that go into our decision making.

The subject is complex and there are no quick, easy, or uniform answers. We're never going to agree with our teen or with one another about what's appropriate with regard to clothes, language, or sexual behavior. And that's a good thing. But we need to have the conversation, to get our kids to think and to offer our guidance in helping them find their own way of making responsible choices.

So What Can I Do with My Sexual Energy?

"So, I get the part about sexual desire being an energy, but what am I supposed to tell my son he's supposed to do with this energy?"

Margaret is the mother of a fourteen-year-old boy. She's recently found a pornographic magazine in the nightstand next to his bed. Margaret does not agree with her religion with regard to sexual behavior, but wants to raise her son to be a responsible sexual adult. The question has two parts to it, and the bigger part is an ethical and perhaps spiritual one: what are you supposed to do, what is the right thing to do, with your sexual energy? Even if Margaret wanted to raise her son to follow the guidelines of her religion she would have to do more than just relate them to her son. If she wanted him to take her seriously she would have to engage him in an ongoing dialogue where they could explore why the guidelines make sense in the world he is living in.

But before we get to how to decide what's the "right" thing to do (covered more fully in Chapter 6), let's take a look at the second part of the question, what is it possible to do. Presenting possibilities to teens and discussing choices is always a good place to begin. When you think about it logically, there are only three things that can be done with sexual energy:

1. You can release sexual energy with another person.
2. You can release sexual energy yourself, by masturbating.
3. You can transform sexual energy into something else.

Releasing Sexual Energy with Someone Else

How one makes the decision to release sexual energy with another person is given an entire chapter (Chapter 6) because it is by far the most complicated choice. If you care about acting responsibly you not only have to consider your own feelings, but also the feelings and well-being of another person. At the most basic level, we should let our kids know that independent of what they see on TV responsible people never use sex to acquire power, either for bragging rights or to gain control over another human being.

Releasing sexual energy with another person can also involve legal and physical risks. The laws in many states forbid any form of sex between people under age fourteen, EVEN IF IT'S CONSENSUAL. Most people don't know this, but the implications are intense. If a thirteen-year-old girl has oral sex with a thirteen-year-old boy of her own free will, and the girl's parents find out, they can charge the boy with statutory rape. The boy's parents can countersue, charging the girl with the same thing. As bizarre as this may sound, it has happened. Sexually transmitted diseases should also be discussed. If you are not familiar with the latest medical information on STDs[2] and have not imparted that information to your teen, they are at risk. Do not assume they got it in health class. Having taught many such classes, I can assure you that given the amount of excitement that accompanies any conversation about sex, the chance of their having retained the information they have been given is small. Information about STDs[3] should be shared a couple of times a year throughout adolescence, verbally as well as in writing.

• •

take it home

1. Become an expert in STDs, how you get them and how you prevent them, and practice explaining this information to your child. Give the information in writing as well. (See notes.)
2. Call your county district attorney's office and have them send you information on the legal consequences of underage sex. Ask your teen what he or she thinks about the law. It's a great conversation starter.

• •

Masturbation—Yes, It's Part of This Discussion

Masturbation is a choice that parents should not hesitate to discuss with their teens. Several religions have rules against masturbation. If this is the case in your faith and you don't want your teen to masturbate, do the research necessary to make sense out of this so that you can help your teen understand the meaning and value behind this restriction. Teens are programmed to question everything, and that's a good thing. We lose credibility as a reliable source of wisdom and information when we rely on religious dogma without understanding it or being willing to discuss and defend it.

Whatever the religious considerations, one should never confuse the issue by telling teens that something bad will happen to them physically if they masturbate. It's appalling the number of kids who still believe that they will go blind or develop acne if they touch themselves. It's not true, and every time we lie we remove ourselves a little bit more from being seen as a source of accurate information and guidance.

There are other considerations one should be aware of when thinking of releasing sexual energy through masturbation, particularly obsessive masturbation to only one kind of stimulation. In my private practice, I've seen men who, having released sexual energy exclusively through masturbation over a prolonged period of time, experience difficulty reaching orgasm within a relationship. There is no current research to support that this is the case with most men; however, the easy access to Internet porn by children makes this a subject worth discussing with teens.

Now this should not be overgeneralized to mean that if a teen masturbates while looking at sexually provocative pictures he will never be able to achieve sexual satisfaction in a loving, mutually pleasing relationship. It does mean that if over a prolonged period of time one only achieves orgasm through masturbating to visual stimulus, one's ability to be stimulated by the more subtle, interpersonal sensations in a relationship with a real human being may be affected. This also would pertain to the kind of visual stimulation that one is using to masturbate. Demeaning pictures or pictures that promote dominance of one person over another can, over time, train a person to respond only to that form of stimulation. Of course, some would say that all pornography is demeaning to all parties involved. I'll leave that conversation to others. As parents, we need to inform our children that the sexual habits you develop now have implications for the quality of sexual relationships and sexual satisfaction that you will enjoy, or not enjoy, later. Just as the eating habits you develop in childhood become the foundation of your eating preferences as an adult, so do the sexual habits you develop in adolescence define your sexual identity and the quality of sexual relationships you have in adulthood. It's really common sense but we don't often think about it. What we do creates who we become—socially, sexually, emotionally, and spiritually.

Transforming the Power of Sexual Energy

Desires are an amazing power source. We will literally move mountains to get what we want. But how do we take the raw energy of desire and turn it into directed action? How do we take the tantrum-throwing two-year-old at the checkout line, who can only dissipate the energy of his desires by having a meltdown, and help him become a self-controlled, goal-directed human being?

We help them develop the muscle to hold the energy of their desires, and then transform that energy into directed action. Developing the muscle to do this is essential to becoming a sexually responsible adult and is addressed fully in Chapter 7.

We start by letting teens know that the energy of our sexual desire can be transformed into other forms of expression. If we are in control of our desire, we can use the energy in an endless number of ways. The energy of unrequited sexual desire has been transformed into the greatest music, art, and literature the world has ever known. The pent-up, stored, and directed energy of sexual passion can be released as violence in war or game-winning tackles on the football field. The coach's old refrain, "No sex before the game," is testament to our intuition that sexual energy can be transformed. If this seems a little abstract for your kids, it's not. Kids get this stuff right away. They can see and feel the result of unrequited sexual desire in the music and movies they watch. They want to know that this energy that can be so overwhelming to them can be put to other uses. I've had guidance counselors, nurses, and parents tell me how delighted kids are to be able to talk about the intensity of their sexual feelings and explore creative ways of using that energy. I remember talking about this with a severely learning-disabled teenage girl. She was having a hard time resisting her boyfriend's advances and couldn't really understand why grown-ups were telling her she wasn't ready for intimacy. She understood the concept of transforming her sexual desire right away. Pulling a notebook from her backpack, she showed me page after page of poems and love letters she had written. "I'm putting all of my sexual energy into this book," she announced. "Then I'll give him the book and that will have to be good enough until I'm older."

Teens are looking for a way to delay sexual activity. They intuitively know that they're not ready. But at the same time they want their newfound sexual energy acknowledged and valued, they want to explore it within guidelines that allow them to feel adventurous and safe.

Science is full of examples of one kind of energy being transformed into another. Somewhere around fifth grade, kids study different kinds of energy. In their textbook's chapter on how electricity is made from hydraulic power, one might find a drawing of a power plant generator at the base of a waterfall and huge electric cables extending out of the power plant, trailing off into the distance, and lighting up a city. Raw hydropower is being transformed or converted into electric power. Raw energy is being controlled and transformed into usable energy that is directed at our will. Kids understand that we are our own power generators. Raw energy, in the form of overwhelming desires, is enormously powerful. Without the transformer, without the muscle of self-control, we can be swept away by our desires. But with tools to transform our energy into directed action, we have the potential to light up the universe.

Abstinence Sounds Like a Diet

So isn't this just another way of selling abstinence? No. Transformation is a positive way of acknowledging and validating the fantastic potential of sexual desire. We can be delighted that we have inherited this power; grateful for the pleasure that sex can bring us, and we can focus on the tools we will need to transform sexual power into creative or physical expression. Abstinence sounds like a diet, like deprivation. Like all diets, it immediately elicits the desire to do the thing we're not supposed to do. If we are introducing sex as a magnificent energy, we have to have equally positive choices as to what they can do with that energy.

From a practical perspective, the abstinence approach is simply less effective. Telling teens they should abstain sets them up to want to do it even more—if not at thirteen years old, then at seventeen. Telling anyone that a release of pleasure is wrong or bad triggers mind games that, even if one abstains, makes doing it even more attractive.

Being able to choose what to do with one's sexual energy, knowing that it's OK, even inspiring, to mold your early passions into creative self-expression until you are ready for greater intimacy is an empowering choice, and it works. This does not mean that we forgo conveying guidelines, religious rules, or our principles. All of these are vital (see Chapter 8). But let's change the way we talk about the choices. How you say something, especially to a teen, can make all the difference.

Acknowledging the Spiritual Dimension

If sexual energy can be converted into creative expression (art, music, literature), physical aggression (sports, war), or procreation (survival of the species), it can also be channeled toward union with the divine. There are many religions worldwide in which celibacy is either required or suggested as a way of directing one's full life energy to the pursuit of union with God. Why not talk about this? Building one's sexual energy while focusing one's mind and behavior on the pursuit of God is an ancient and, for some, an inspiring quest. History is replete with stories of spiritual heroes who have directed their entire life energy, including sexual energy, toward service to and union with God. Members of many different religious affiliations see this life choice as the highest expression of one's sexuality. Agree or disagree, think about whether discussing why people make these choices would be helpful to your teen.

Is Sexual Energy Different If You're Gay?

Often parents of gay teens will approach me after a lecture and ask me how this way of talking about sex relates to gay teens. Learning how to control and direct our sexual energy in a responsible and ethical manner relates equally to everyone who experiences sexual desire.

What about the emphasis that's placed on understanding the source of sexual desire as a biological drive toward procreation and the continuation of the species? Homosexual sex cannot result in procreation, so how does this relate?

As a species, we are driven toward sex because that is how procreation happens; however, as individuals we have sexual desire independent of whether or not we want to conceive a child. Similarly, even if we are not capable of conceiving a child, many of us will experience a time in our life when we choose to direct our sexual energy toward finding a mate, and creating a protective family unit that can nurture children. This choice to spend our energy contributing to the well-being of the next generation is not dependent on our physical ability to procreate or on our sexual orientation.

More to the point of talking to teens about sex is understanding that, independent of sexual orientation, their sexual energy is overwhelming and easily manipulated. Talking to teens about developing the self-discipline to control and direct the energy of their desires and to act toward others in a responsible and ethical way is just common sense. There is a great deal to be said, however, about how we fail to teach our kids the fundamentals of compassionate behavior.

Living in a World Where Anything Can Make You Gay

During puberty, when everyone is struggling to form a social/sexual identity, the one thing most kids unite around is that no one wants to be labeled "gay." How could they, since calling someone gay as a put-down starts as early as first grade. Even at that age, when many children have no idea what it means, they already associate it with social isolation.

A few years ago, I was giving a presentation to a group of sixth graders, when one of the students told me that on picture day, she had worn a yellow sweater to school.

"All of my friends told me I had to call my mom and have her bring in a different shirt. They said that if I wore yellow everyone who saw that picture would think I was gay."

"So if you wear yellow you're gay?" I asked.

A boy pitched in, "Someone called me gay because I brought Jell-O for lunch."

What followed was a laundry list of clothes and foods and actions that changed from day to day that could be brought out at the whim of the powerful and used to isolate a child by labeling them gay. I kept wondering what was going through the mind of the child who was listening to all this thinking, "that's me."

I don't address issues of homosexuality in public schools because I embrace the principle that respecting diversity means respecting those parents whose religious convictions are opposed to homosexuality. I let children know that different religions have different understandings about homosexuality and out of respect for all religions represented in the class, homosexuality is something they need to talk with their parents about. I ask them to think about how many times they have heard the word "gay" used to humiliate or isolate someone. I tell them that teen boys who realize they are homosexual are six times more likely to kill themselves than heterosexual males. Gay females are twice as likely.[4] I also tell them that no religion has ever supported humiliating, disrespecting, or harming another human being and that the word "gay" should never be used as a put-down, not even as a "joke."

Parents, teachers, health professionals, school administrators, none of us can afford to have words like "gay," "faggot," "homo," or "lesbo" be words that we overlook when we're teaching our kids the value of respecting all human beings.[5] Can any of us call ourselves compassionate human beings and then fail to stop our children from taunting, humiliating, and assaulting homosexuals?

Feeling the power of our sexual desire is a magnificent human experience. At the heart of this miraculous power lies the potential to create a human being. This power can bring us great pleasure. It can be transformed into exquisite physical and creative expression. When we learn how to acknowledge the power of our children's desires; when we give them the tools to control, direct, and transform that power, we give them the ability to choose to act responsibly.

••

take it home

1. Watch TV with your teen and find the ways advertisers use sex, or the hope of becoming sexy, to manipulate you.
2. Watch a reality TV show together and count the ways sex is used to manipulate others.
3. Is it ever OK for people to use their sexual power to get what they want? What does your child think?

••

five

·················

Self-Discipline: Developing the Muscle to Say No to Something That Feels Good

becoming a responsible sexual adult starts with understanding that sexuality is an energy that we learn to control and direct in a responsible manner. As our bodies begin to transform into adult bodies, our senses start to respond to sexually stimulating cues in our environment, activating the energy of our desire. As parents, we hope that our children will choose to use this energy in a way that aligns with the values we've taught them (see Chapter 8). But too often I see children who have been taught responsible behavior, who can articulate very wisely how they want to conduct themselves, but in that moment, when they are filled with desire, are unable to act on their values. What's missing?

Whether it's sexual desire or the desire to eat a second helping of cheesecake, if we can't stop ourselves from immediately gratifying the demands of our senses, all the good intentions and values in the world won't help. Our children need to understand how the environment that they choose to live in has the power to activate their desires. Once activated, our kids need the internal muscle to stop and assess whether they want to act on their desires or redirect that energy in another way. The best gift we can give our children is helping them develop the muscle to pause when their desires are activated and choose how they want to release the energy of their desires. To have the strength to pause when your senses are demanding gratification, to be able to hold that energy and to choose how you want to use it, is to have developed the muscle of self-discipline.

Self-discipline is a prerequisite for remaining healthy in every aspect of our lives. But with the risk of AIDS and the prevalence of alcohol abuse among teens, sex is a part of our lives where having self-discipline is critical. Unfortunately there is little in our consumer-driven culture that positively reinforces us for saying no to that which is pleasurable.

Teaching the Value of Self-Discipline in a Culture Where More Is Always Better

There is no limit to what we can have in America. From shampoo to sneakers, iPods to toothpaste, the choices are limitless. Our children are inundated with the promise of happiness and success if only they can convince us to buy them that one thing they really want. Not only will they be happy, but they will also be sexy, successful, beautiful, and admired. Watch a Saturday morning's worth of children's programming. There's more than product being sold. The values being taught align happiness with immediate gratification of desire. Getting what you want is your inalienable right. Bigger is always better. It's how much you have that defines you and tells the world how successful you are. These same consumer principals are now being applied to sex. College students make booty calls on a Saturday night as if sex were a product to be ordered in like a pizza. Middle school girls and boys brag about their hookups as if they were products to be acquired. At the all-you-can-eat buffet of American culture, too often we let our kids define themselves by how much of everything they can shove onto their plate. If we want something more for our children, if we understand that being dragged around by our latest desire is no prescription for happiness, than we will teach them the value of self-discipline.

We begin by helping our children understand that, despite what they see on TV, success is not a sum game. We show them that defining ourselves by how much we can get or by how quickly we can satisfy our desires, although good for the economy, leaves us unprepared to follow the values we believe in. True success is having the discrimination and self-discipline to align our choices with our goals and values. What we choose *not* to take at the buffet of life defines us as much as what we take. Having the strength to say no to things even when we want them gives us the freedom to choose what's important to us and the power to act on our choices. Teens and young adults are not ready to make responsible sexual decisions until they have developed the muscle to stop and evaluate whether or not it is in their best interest to satisfy their desires. The teens and children I work with are hungry to understand that their desires are a huge source of power that they can learn to control and direct. They want to develop the muscle to exercise choice.

Developing the Muscle of Self-Discipline

When we allow ourselves to feel the power of desire, our bodies literally pulsate with energy, moving toward satisfying the desire. When we hold that energy in check, we call it delaying gratification. It takes practice to develop the muscle to hold that energy, to stop before acting on our desires. Teaching self-discipline starts when we validate the power of our children's desires. The muscle of self-discipline holds that power in check and gives us time to figure out what we want to do with that energy.

When our children are young *we* restrain their behavior, in effect becoming their self-discipline until they are old enough to begin to develop this muscle themselves. Talking about how our senses are activated, helping them understand how desires are a form of energy, and giving them ways to demonstrate that they are in control of that energy helps them internalize the value of self-discipline. The challenge of parenting is to find age-appropriate ways of helping our kids develop this muscle.

Desires Are Great!

The first step in helping our children learn to control their desires is by not presenting desire as something bad. Desire is great! It is the source of enormous energy. Instead, we help our children become aware of this energy by talking with them about the power of their desires. Then we subtly challenge them to be strong enough to hold this energy, even for a few minutes.

Imagine you're picking your child up from school and you have forgotten to bring a snack.

CHILD: I'm starving, Mom!

MOM: You are really hungry!

CHILD: I need to eat right now!

MOM: Being hungry is a very powerful feeling. On a scale of one to ten, how powerful is your desire for food?

CHILD: It's a twelve!

MOM: Oh, my goodness. You would have to be very strong to hold a twelve! What does all that power feel like?

CHILD: It feels like I'm so hungry I could jump out of the car and run home to get food myself!

MOM: That is a lot of energy! I bet it would be hard to hold that much energy in your body for even one minute.

CHILD: I could hold it for five minutes!

MOM: Five minutes is a long time. A twelve is a powerful desire.

CHILD: I mean it, Mom. I could hold it for five minutes. No problem.

MOM: Well, it's already been one minute. I'm impressed. It can be hard to hold the energy of hunger. You're doing great!

It's the muscle of self-discipline that lets us hold the energy of our desires. With a little imagination, we can also teach our kids how to transform that energy.

MOM: I'm amazed that you can hold your energy for that long. I'm wondering if you can use that energy for something.

CHILD: I want to use it to eat something.

MOM: I know, but since we can't do that right now, what about changing it into a song? Why not use your energy to create a song?

CHILD: (singing) I'm so hungry I might die, I might cry, I might fly to the sky. . . .

MOM: I can't believe how great you are at using your hunger energy to create something. That song was amazing!

We teach self-discipline by:

- Letting kids know that desire is great! We acknowledge how powerful desire is and begin to access how much energy desire gives you (scale of one to ten).
- Acknowledging how strong you have to be to hold the energy of your desires.
- Learning to transform the energy of wanting into the power of work or creative expression.
- Looking for opportunities to challenge children to hold and transform their energy in ways that fit their age and abilities.
- Admiring and supporting their efforts.

With Older Kids, We Can Talk About Work

How we talk about the energy of our desires, and what we can do with that energy, changes as our children get older. The snack-in-the-car routine is great with younger children. With older kids, we can continue to teach them how to hold and transform the energy of their desires by using their delight in being productive as well as their natural curiosity about "work."

Assuming we haven't inherited a trust fund, most of us have figured out ways to turn the energy of wanting something into the effort, or work, of getting it. If we want a car, we get a job, work hard, get money, and buy the car. We transform the energy of our desire into work and are rewarded by that sweet feeling of satisfaction when we get what we want. Our whole culture runs on the cycle of **wanting ➜ working ➜ getting ➜ and wanting more.** We can even think of money as a tangible form of effort, little packets of energy we've transformed into a usable form of power. Successful people are often those who have developed the muscle of self-control and know how to store the energy of desire and transform it into work. They've learned how to delay gratification long enough to save those wonderful little packets of energy we call money. By storing the power that comes from accumulating this energy, they can become more powerful, more able to choose how they want to expend their energy. When they think about desire and energy as precursors to money and wealth, older kids are motivated to develop the muscle of self-discipline.

When It Comes to Sex, Being Safe Is About Information and Self-Discipline

An important part of any sexuality curriculum is understanding how to protect oneself from sexually transmitted diseases, particularly AIDS. In my class, I forcefully drive home the point that AIDS is a deadly disease. At the same time, I tell the class that they do not have to worry about getting AIDS as long as they have two things: information and self-discipline.

Information is something I can give them, but self-discipline is a muscle that they have to develop themselves. No amount of information is going to protect them from AIDS if they haven't developed the muscle to say no to something that feels good. How do you do that? You start by first practicing holding the energy of your desires, and intentionally delaying gratification, slowly building the muscle of self-discipline.

Since I've already introduced sex as energy powerful enough to allow us to survive as a species, it is a logical next step to understand that the muscle needed to control and use this energy responsibly must be equally powerful.

When talking about desire with preteens, it helps to give them examples and exercises that they can relate to *before* they've actually experienced sexual desire. I use hunger because it's a simple desire that I can manipulate in the classroom. I ask the class to rank how hungry they are on a scale of one to ten. Then I manipulate their desire by taking them through this imaginary exercise.

"Imagine that your mother picks you up from school today and tells you that she's going to stop at your favorite bakery and buy you anything you want. Ummm! Think about what you're going to get. So, you're driving there and you're thinking about what you're going to pick and now you see the bakery in the distance. Your mom pulls up, parks, and you follow her in. As you walk through the door, you can smell the pastries. On a scale of one to ten, how hungry are you now?

"So now you're in line, waiting to be served. You can see your special treat sitting there behind the glass counter, waiting for you. How hungry are you now? You finally get to the front of the line and your mom asks you what you want. The lady behind the counter puts it in the bag and you can't wait to take it back to the car. Your mom completes her order and reaches into her pocketbook and discovers . . . she's forgotten her wallet."

At this point everyone in the class lets out an enormous groan.

"Did you hear that sound you just made?" I ask. "That sound is the energy of your desires. The energy that I manipulated by simply having you imagine something that you wanted. Everyone has seen a baby have a tantrum. When babies can't get what they want, there's an explosion of energy. They haven't learned how to hold and direct the energy of their desires. Holding the energy of desire is one form of self-discipline. Sometimes you exercise self-discipline by pushing yourself to do something past the point when it's easy. Other times you exercise self-discipline by holding the energy of your desires, letting it build, and using it in another way."

I then ask the class to pick one thing that they really like doing, such as having a snack after school or watching a favorite television show. I tell them that their homework is to test their muscle by deciding not to have or do the thing they want. I ask them to write down what it feels like to let the energy build inside of them and how it feels to consciously hold that energy. Together, we imagine ways they can use their built-up energy. We talk about work, practicing sports, and creating art as ways they can transform their energy.

Then we get back to AIDS. Sexual desire is one of the most powerful energies there is. I am very clear that no matter how smart they are, no matter how much they can learn about HIV and AIDS, they can never feel safe if they have not developed the muscle of self-discipline. I let each of them know that by developing that muscle now, they will build the confidence they need to choose whether to release or hold their sexual energy.

take it home

When everyone is seated at the dinner table ready to dive in,
stop. Tell everyone that you're conducting an experiment. Before eating, have everyone sit in silence for two full minutes,
letting the energy of desire for the food build. Ask them to
note how it feels to smell, and see, and think about the food,
but decide not to eat the food. After two minutes (much short-
er for very young children), take a slow, thoughtful bite of
food and really taste it. Discuss as a family what the sensation
of waiting was like. Could they feel the energy building? What
could they accomplish with that energy? Was that first bite
different because they waited? How was it different? Which of
their senses contributed the most to the building of their desire? Begin a conversation about the muscle of self-discipline.
Ask them if they know any kids who could really use more of
that muscle and why they think so.

Drugs and Alcohol Obliterate Self-Discipline

This way of talking about self-discipline provides an easy bridge
to understanding the hazards of drugs and alcohol, which obliter-
ate self-discipline.

The brain is our command center, the ultimate decision maker.
At the moment when our senses are demanding release of energy,
it is the brain that chooses our action and directs the body to exercise the muscle of self-discipline. The brain ultimately sends

the message to stop, overriding the body's desires. But what if terrorists enter the command center and contaminate it with toxins? What if the command center has been sabotaged and can no longer issue a stop order? We know that sexual behavior at an early age is often linked to experimentation with drugs and alcohol.[1] We know that alcohol is a huge part of the hookup scene in high school and college. I talk with parents who just accept this as a given, allowing kids to drink in their home because, "I know they're going to do it anyway, so I might as well be where I can keep an eye on them." Apart from being illegal, it would seem relevant to ask our kids, and ourselves, why we have come to equate happiness with turning off the command center.

Many kids as young as middle school age talk about the pressure they feel to perform during the week, and the hours of homework and relentless critiquing of their performance from parents and educators. Weekends are the antidote, made for obliterating consciousness. They feel they've earned the right to shut down their executive functioning. I've had high school teachers and administrators tell me that it's impossible to get anything accomplished on Mondays because of the level of partying that takes place over the weekend. There is an entire book to be written about how we can bring a greater awareness of balance and consciousness into our children's lives. When it comes to talking with kids about sex, it is imperative to discuss the effects of drugs on their decision making.

Most of us know the right thing to do. Our parents, teachers, and religious leaders have taught us what it means to be a good person. Where many of us fall short is having the inner muscle *to do* the things we know we're supposed to do and *not to do* the things that we know are unhealthy or unethical. As parents, we do our best to convey the principles of moral/ethical behavior to our children. But somewhere in the hurriedness of our day and in the abundance of our culture, we have spent less time helping our kids understand that being proud of yourself is not just about how much you can get, but also about what you choose *not* to have.

Helping kids develop the muscle of self-discipline gives them the freedom to choose those things that will truly make them happy. When it comes to sex, self-discipline gives them the ability to choose based on their principles, not their desires. In a world of HIV and AIDS, self-discipline is the tool they need to stay safe.

....

six

When It Comes to Sex and Teens, Talking Isn't Enough

i cannot BELIEVE that you are going to make me change my clothes!" That's my daughter. I think. But not the daughter I actually know, the one I can talk to, not the one who is bright and sensitive and able to understand the fine nuances of human interaction much better than most adults I know. I have no idea what's happened to her. The daughter standing in front of me with one hand on her hip and that cold, detached glare in her eye is wrapped in an attitude so thick she looks like some caricature of herself. Rational conversation has been temporarily suspended.

Even if we have the foresight to start talking to our child about sex and sexuality before they reach puberty, when the hormones kick in, the dialogue changes. Gone are the days when our words fall on receptive ears. The child who was available, who wanted to be with us, and who was more or less responsive to our guidance has begun transforming into a fully sexualized adult. Teens' job during adolescence is to acquire the skills, as well as the emotional distance they need, to leave us and eventually, if they choose, establish a family of their own. Our job is to get them through this transformation in one piece, with a set of values they can be proud of, and maintain our sanity.

Who *are* these people who are suddenly so annoyed with us? Why are they compelled to disagree with everything we say? When did being with their friends become such an obsession?

Many parents who felt confident parenting babies, toddlers, and children become unglued when faced with a self-absorbed, argumentative teen. The parenting skills we've used successfully for twelve or thirteen years are suddenly ineffective in influencing (or even engaging) whoever has come to inhabit our child's body. As they swing, willy-nilly, between sagelike maturity and juvenile inanity, we try to keep up by imposing too little structure one minute and over-the-top restrictions that we have no way of enforcing the next. Swept up in the drama, we can exhaust ourselves trying to figure out when to say no to our teen and when to allow more independence.

Making sexually responsible decisions involves many different facets of our teens' lives. How much our teens need to belong, the behavior of their friends, and the choices they make about drugs and alcohol will all impact whether or not and under what conditions they choose to express their sexuality. The parenting choices *we* make—as we weather their constant demands for more freedom—can be more important than what we say. All of our talk about sex won't help if our teens find themselves in situations that they are not emotionally ready to handle.

As the tsunami of adolescence swirls around our children, we have to structure their exploration and growing independence in a way that allows them to stay safe. It helps to pause, take a look at where we tend to get stuck, develop strategies to help us stay focused on our goal, and examine how our role needs to change as we make that final push to successfully birth our child into adulthood.

Remember Labor and Multiply by Ten

Let's face it: we're in labor all over again. The first time, we birthed our children into existence; now we're birthing them into adulthood. Amazingly, it is the same set of hormones that triggered labor years ago that is now working its magic on our teens, growing them into adults capable of reproducing and starting this whole process again. This second labor begins with that first whiff of body odor and doesn't end until they move out of the house. It helps to have the support of other adults, extended family at times, and professionals who work well with teens.

In family therapy, teens are often seen as "the problem." I see the family as a system (or body) of interlocking cells preparing to give birth. The teenage member of the family, often sitting off to one side in sulking agitation, is in a state of transformation into an adult body. This process vibrates through the whole family system. What nobody can see, because they are inside the family cluster, is that this restless teen is preparing to break free, and the rest of the family is in intense labor. I'm the birthing coach. I've got to help everyone see what's going on and help the parents *keep their eye on the goal of successfully launching this cell out into the world where it can someday create a family of its own.* Each family member has a unique role to play.

The anger, the attitude, the ridiculous argumentativeness, the fighting, the door slamming, and the unbearable frustration are all labor contractions. The birthing process begins sometime around age eleven or twelve with a little confrontation, eye rolling, lack of interest in being with us, but just as quickly they return, acting overly needy and dependent. It's as if the idea of being born into adulthood has scared them and they want to crawl back inside. This is false labor, a few Braxton Hicks to prepare us for things to come. So how do you know when real labor has begun? You find yourself entertaining the idea that having them gone might be an enormous relief. Horrified, you push the thought away, but it returns again and again, intensifying as the labor dance unfolds.

Becoming Part of the Next Generation

By age thirteen or fourteen, *our* words and ideas have begun to wane in comparison with those of their peers. Our teens have started to embrace the job of leaving. Breaking free of us involves finding their own way of thinking and feeling about things. They are driven to acquire some sense of themselves and to attain a level of confidence that they can make it without us. Initially, they try to establish an identity by finding their place in the culture of their peers. They struggle to find out how they fit in the hierarchy of the next generation.

Recently, I dropped my son and daughter off at school. I hadn't done this in several months, as their father usually takes them to school. As Zach opened the car door, I turned and said, "Bye, bye, sweetie, have a great day!" and reached to give him a hug. My daughter looked at me in horror.

"Mom," she said, "no one talks to Zach after he opens the door."

"No one talks to Zach after he opens the door?" I repeated

lamely, turning to my son. Still seated, he closed the car door and looked at me.

"OK, Mom, say what you have to say," he said with forced indulgence.

"Right," I said, "I guess that means a hug is out."

He just stared at me.

"Have a great day."

"Yeah, you too, Mom."

Then he straightened his shirt, took one last look in the mirror, plugged himself into his music thing, and left.

It was amazing! In the car he was a child, my son, a brother. But the moment the car door opened, his membership shifted from family to peers. This shift took concentration: the look, the style, the attitude, and the props all had to be just right. Fully accessorized, armor in place, he could unplug from the family unit and plug into his own generation. What a huge amount of work!

When we look at our teen, we're looking at a fledgling member of the next generation: doing everything he or she can to separate from us by establishing a group identity with his or her own generation. Membership is defined by one's ability to adopt the music, fashion, language, style, and attitude of one's peers. Teens are always assessing how well they fit this new group identity, whether in the lunchroom, the mall, or online. As one teen put it when I asked how she figures out what is cool, "I just go to the mall and see how all the other kids are."

Have you ever watched and listened to a group of teens? They talk about absolutely nothing. They laugh about nothing. They mumble and push and giggle at each other and absorb each other's company. Have you ever spent time with your own teen after he or she has been with other teens? That's when things get dicey. The lovely son or daughter you dropped off at the party is a stranger when he or she reenters the family unit. It's as if they've become someone else. And they have. They've become members of the next generation.

Don't Get Derailed by Attitude

Initiating a discussion about sex is hard enough, but when faced with the eye-rolling, "Oh-my-God-I-can't-believe-you're-going-to-talk-to-me-about-that-stuff! I-have-heard-this-a-million-times-in-health-class!" teen, it's tempting to put it off, hoping for a better opportunity. It pays to become versed in teen attitude so that we don't let it keep us from doing our job.

Without warning, "attitude" can descend over teens like a brittle facade. Their movements become almost stylized, their voices can fluctuate between something resembling a cat's hiss and a mumbly, mush-mouth swamp sound where not one word is comprehensible. My daughter, lover of all that is dramatic, leans more toward the cat.

My son's attitude is completely different. He takes on the angry loner facade, head down, voice in a perpetual mumble, no eye contact, as if living itself is a wretchedly unfair joke and having to interact with me is the worst part of all. It goes like this:

"Do you have homework tonight?"

Silence.

"Zach, do you have homework tonight?"

"What?" (Now understand, he's sitting next to me in the front seat of the car.)

"Do you have any homework?"

"Idonwannatshabutit."

"What?"

"Idonwannatchbutit."

"I don't understand you."

"What?"

"I can't understand what you're saying."

"What do you mean?"

"I mean, I don't understand what you just said."

"Not really."

"Not really, what?"

"Not really. You asked me a question and I'm saying 'not really.'"

"You 'don't really' have any homework?"

"Kinda, but not really."

"What does that mean, 'kinda, but not really'?" (Now my voice is rising.)

"Why are you yelling at me?"

"I'm not yelling at you!" (I'm yelling.)

"I can't talk to you if you're going to yell."

You get the drift.

On my good days, I transcend these moments by imagining I'm in a situation comedy about how it feels to live with teens. This is the part where the audience is laughing at the complete absurdity of it all, I think, as I bite my lip and take a deep breath.

Sometimes I become crazed and yell, "IT'S A SIMPLE QUESTION! DO YOU HAVE ANY HOMEWORK?"

Somewhere in my beleaguered brain, I realize he is using his mush-mouth, dopey attitude to distance from me. By pushing me into that quicksand of utter noncommunication, eventually I will simply be too exhausted to go on. And he's right. What are my choices? If I do what he seems to want me to do, turn on the radio and give up, he's effectively pushed me away. If I let my anger overwhelm me and turn into crazed, authoritarian mom from hell, screaming about responsibility, communication, and blah, blah, blah, I end any possibility of connection and he has effectively pushed me away. What is the goal here, and why do I repeat this cycle over and over? His intention, conscious or not, is to distance from me, to remove himself from my domain of influence.

The weird irony here is that despite all their infuriating distancing techniques, teens actually do want us to keep talking. Even when it comes to talking about sex, research repeatedly shows that teens want to hear what we have to say,[1] they want to know our values, and at the same time, they are hardwired to never, ever let us know. Understanding why teens *need* their attitude can help us persevere and remember that the job of parenting a teen does not come with much immediate positive reinforcement.

Stop Trying to Convince Them; They're Not Supposed to Agree

As much as teens say that they want to hear what we think about sex and sexual behavior, more often than not they will resist listening, flood you with attitude, and disagree with everything you say. (If you want to have a conversation, try a long car ride and leave the cell phones and iPods at home.) Successfully birthing a teen into adulthood depends on understanding that conflict is part of the process, and that their role in the birth often stands in opposition to ours. We can never *expect* to be on the same page. That's just the way it is. They push the envelope. We keep talking and create a structure made up of expectations and consequences where they can safely test their independence. They push some more. We hold the line and stay attentive to their developing maturity, always ready to adjust the structure as they demonstrate responsibility.

It helps me to remember that sometimes the best results come when people play opposing roles. Think of the American legal system. Even if the defense attorney knows his client is guilty, he must play his part and defend him. At the same time, the prosecuting attorney would never acknowledge that the defendant might be innocent. His job is to get the jury to convict. Messy as it is, our legal system works best when everyone plays his or her part.

Too often, I see parents who think they should be able to convince their teen to act responsibly. When talking doesn't work, they become frustrated, hurt, and confused. They've forgotten that teens are supposed to disagree, push the envelope, and try to convince us that they're mature enough to do things they are not mature enough to do. That's *their* part in the dance of separation. We're supposed to be prepared for their attitude, be clear about our expectations, be prepared with consequences if necessary, and accept that often we will not agree.

On family vacation, I asked my daughter to change her clothes for a particularly formal event. She and a friend had just spent several hours with a group of teens and she was covered in attitude. "I don't have a skirt," she told me, straight-faced, looking me in the eye. "I don't have anything 'appropriate' to wear." Less than two weeks earlier, the two of us had gone shopping for this particular event. She had picked out a beautiful skirt, which she had dearly loved, and I had been with her when she had put it in her suitcase. What was she thinking? "Do you have any idea where you are or who you are talking to?" I asked, with complete bafflement. She looked at her friend, rolled her eyes, and walked away to get changed. I felt like I'd just stepped into the twilight zone.

As completely unlike her as this whole episode was, it would be unfair to hope that she would help me do *my* job. Our roles are, by definition, in opposition to each other. She has to push; I have to hold the structure for her to push against. When we get this, we don't waste our time becoming crazed because our teens are not in alignment with us. (Hoping to have our teen on the same page is like having the prosecuting attorney get angry because the defense attorney is claiming the defendant is innocent.) The system works best *because* we play different roles. Our teens can't do our job, and we can't do theirs.

So does that mean we stop talking to them about why we are expecting them to act in a particular way? ABSOLUTELY NOT! Talk, and talk, and talk, and talk despite the eye rolling and the huffing and puffing and all the rest. We know our words are very important to them, even as they walk away and slam the door. That said, we shouldn't fool ourselves into thinking we've done anything terribly effective. Talking is like treading water. You haven't drowned, but you're no closer to shore. You just haven't given up. Effectiveness comes when you are smart enough to structure their opportunities so that life gently teaches them the lessons they need to learn.

• •

take it home

1. Can you remember a time when your teen insisted on disagreeing with you even though you could tell that he or she didn't really believe what he or she was saying? Ask your parent if you ever did the same thing.

2. Think of a time when you tried to get your teen to agree with the restrictions or guidelines you placed on him or her. Did it work?

3. Do you get angry when you can't convince your teen that you are right? What happens when you get angry?

• •

Creating a Structure Teens Can Push Against

Listen to Ann and Sara, two sixth graders who are working out a strategy for how they might remain cool while refusing to go to a party where they know there will be drugs, alcohol, and sex.

"I know! I could say that I've got a really mean father who would totally kill me if he found out."

"That's good for you because your dad is like, really intense, but what could I say?"

"You could lie and say you have a tough dad."[2]

On the night of the party, these two girls will be begging their parents to let them go. Why? They are biologically driven to push against us. We would all like to imagine that our son or daughter would be the one who chooses not to go to the party and, yes, there are a few kids who will make that choice. But think about what we're asking. Every cell in their body is aching for acceptance by their peers, terrified that they will be isolated or made fun of. They have to try and convince us to go even if they don't want to.

Unlike the first birth, which took place in a hospital with a legion of professionals waiting to assist, this transition to adulthood happens in a consumer-led culture of peers where "freedom" and "individuality" are expressed by conforming to the style, language, music, drugs, and sexual norms of their generation. There is an entire book to be written about how adults can better help teens direct this push toward independence, but a great deal can be learned by looking carefully at this tidbit of conversation between these two sixth-grade girls. They are fantasizing about having a structure to push against, imagining the tough parent who will give them a way *to save face and stay safe*. They are giving us information we need to play our part in the birthing process.

A structure is something that parents put into place so that we don't have to rehash the same old stuff with every new demand. In the busyness of our day-to-day lives, structure saves us from succumbing to a demand for freedom that, if we had time to think, we would know they're not ready for.

Let's say our thirteen-year-old has been invited to a party. Having a parenting structure in place means that before your teen even asks to go they already know that:

- My parents always ask who is having the party and call first to make sure a parent will be there. When my parents don't know the family, I know they will ask the parents in charge whether there will be alcohol at the party and whether there will be parental supervision for the entire time.
- My parents have let me know exactly what they expect me to do if there are drugs or alcohol at the party, or if an adult is not present.
- I have a curfew and know the consequences if I break curfew.
- If a teenager is picking me up, my parents will insist that the driver come to the door and meet my parents first. Then I have to stand there and listen while my mom or dad lets the driver know both the curfew and driving expectations.
- I know exactly what will happen if I do not meet my parents' expectations.

Creating this structure will not endear you to your child and will probably make you feel ridiculously old. Do it anyway. When we have a structure in place right from the beginning, even when they complain, they understand that this is just the way things are done. The structure has flexibility built in. As they get closer to leaving home and have shown that they can make good choices, you allow them more freedom. As you're deciding on what degree of structure is right for you and your child, remember that it's much easier to give more freedom when it's been earned than to take it back.

Guidelines for Creating Structure

"Why *can't* I have the car?" "What do you mean I can't wear this?" "Everyone's going!" "Other parents don't . . ." and on and on. Who has the presence of mind to sort out things in the moment? It can feel like we're always flying by the seat of our pants, responding to the next demand from a state of fear, anxiety, hurriedness, or exhaustion. We haven't had time to think it through and our kids are more than capable of taking full advantage. After all, that's their job.

Structure sets expectations and guidelines for behavior—while at the same time giving teens sufficient freedom to test themselves and explore their independence. But how do we decide how much structure and how much freedom to give?

Be proactive. Sit down with your partner or another parent and talk through where you stand. Remember that starting out with a lot of structure and later loosening the reins is a great deal easier than taking back freedoms you've already given. It also helps to have an overriding goal that you can hang on to when the pressure is on. Your goal might look something like this:

"I will successfully launch my child into the world as a healthy and responsible adult with values they can be proud of."

This might seem self-evident, but in the moment when we're being badgered to death about a boy/girl sleepover that will make or break their social life, it helps to keep the big picture in mind. Ask yourself, Is my answer to my teen's most recent demand in alignment with my goal? If it's out of the ballpark, just say no.

But what about when you're not quite sure? Maybe they *are* ready for more freedom. After all, it's not like when they leave home they're going to be entering a monastery. Chances are that they'll be at college having to negotiate a mixed-gender dormitory where excessive drinking and sexual exploration is standard fare.[3] Assessing our teen's maturity is very difficult. We can start by asking ourselves these questions:

1. Do they know how to assess whether or not the situation is safe?
2. Can they tell if someone is inebriated or high?
3. Do they understand the effects that drugs and alcohol have on sexual behavior?
4. Have I walked them through the steps they should take if they do not feel safe? Are they capable of following those steps?
5. Do they understand my values and guidelines for behavior? Have they demonstrated that they are capable of following them?
6. How vulnerable are they to peer pressure? Do I know the kids they are hanging out with? Do I like them?
7. Have they developed the muscle of self-discipline? Do they have the ability to say no to something that feels good?

8. Have they had the experience of feeling proud of themselves for doing something difficult?

Understanding that we can never fully know the answers to these questions, the structure we create around our teen will reflect our best guess at any given moment. As they mature, hopefully the answers will reflect a greater level of responsibility and we can loosen the structure. Talking alone won't prepare them. They need to have opportunities to test their convictions and their sense of themselves as a sexual person in situations where they have to make choices. At thirteen years old they are not ready to do that; by seventeen, they had better be.

What Happens If Expectations Are Not Met?

Structure is nothing more than a series of well-defined expectations. But what happens when expectations are not met? What are the consequences for not living up to expectations? Always start positive. Act as if you know the expectations will be met, understanding that you can always deal with consequences if needed. That doesn't mean you haven't thought through in advance what the consequences will be; you've just chosen to project the positive.

Consequences, when delivered, should be immediate, short-lived, and memorably unpleasant. They should reflect the lack of responsibility the teen has shown in dealing with the freedom they've been allowed. In other words, if demonstrating responsibility opens the door to more freedom and independence, then demonstrating a lack of responsibility means having less freedom and independence. If possible, take away the thing they have abused.

contract for safety

The one exception to this is the contract for safety that every parent should make with his or her teen. One of the leading causes of death among teens is drunk driving.[4] One way that each of us can participate in reducing that statistic is to sit down with our teen and create a contract that says, "If you are ever in a situation where you feel unsafe, when you have been drinking or doing drugs, or when the person whom you were depending on to drive you home has been drinking or doing drugs, then you can call me and I will pick you up, *no questions asked.*" The "no questions asked" part may seem counterproductive when it comes to teaching our kids the consequences of unsafe and illegal behavior. But to skip this conversation and this contract is to risk something far worse. Smart, high-functioning kids come into my office every day reciting stories of driving drunk or being driven by someone who was high. Often, they have engaged in some sexual activity that they "really didn't think they wanted to do" but were not able to figure out how to get out of the situation. More often than not, alcohol is involved. I pray every night that each of them lives long enough to remember how stupid they've been. Contracts work. Make one with your teen[5] (see sample contract, Appendix 1).

Take Pride in Being Annoying

To the extent that you impose structure on their lives, you will be seen as utterly annoying. Take it as a compliment. The most common word I hear in my private practice is "annoying." "My parents are sooo annoying!" (and two minutes later) "Did I tell you how annoying my mom is?" Kids with extraordinary intelligence and vocabulary can spend an entire hour repeating that one word. When parents are annoying, I know the prognosis is good. There are a lot more things that can still go wrong, but at least I know that someone is structuring the child's opportunities and doing his or her job.

Most of us can remember our parents being annoying and out of touch to some degree. But if you want an immediate mini-experience of how your teen feels, get in your car and drive onto the interstate. If the speed limit is 60 mph, do you go 60 mph? Many of us will feel comfortable at 70 and flirt with 80, all the while watching for speed traps. Set the limit at 70 mph and we'll go 80. Most of us decide that we are perfectly fine going faster than the law allows, but don't push too much over ten miles above the limit. Why? Because we know those speed traps are there. In those few places where there are no limits, people do not self-monitor but really push way past what is safe. This is human nature. Set the bar and expect people to push against the limits. Set the bar higher, people push even further. And if this is true of adults who supposedly operate with all their brain cells and seminormal hormones, imagine what it feels like to a teen. Unfortunately, we have the unpleasant job of not only setting the speed limits but also setting the speed traps, figuring out at what point we prosecute, and following through on the consequences. To make matters worse, all teens are not the same and even the same teen, minute by minute, is changing and hopefully maturing. A reasonable limit at fourteen years old should be expanded as they demonstrate that they can act responsibly.

How relevant would it be if a police officer sat down with you at breakfast and talked with you about the hazards of speeding? It might impact your driving for the first ten to fifteen minutes you're in the car. And then? It's not that we wouldn't believe the police officer, but in the moment of driving, most of us feel that we can decide what's safe for us while keeping an eye out for the speed traps. Keep this in mind when you're talking to your teen. The words come in and the words go out, but it's the speed traps—and the awareness that the speed traps will always be there—that keep them safe.

It's Not About *Not* Trusting Them, It's Just About Doing Your Job

It's hard to say no. It's hard to feel old. It's hard to sound like your parents. And who knows, maybe you really have ruined their last chance at a social life. Is it really worth all the drama we're going to have to deal with? Ultimately the decision is up to you. The structure I place around my kids reflects my values, my level of anxiety, my best assessment of my kids' maturity, and—to be perfectly honest—the amount of time I have to put into the job at any given moment. The structure you develop will reflect your values and the maturity level of your child. As we try to implement the structure, it helps to remind ourselves that not only are they *not* going to agree with us, they're not supposed to agree. And it is not our job to convince them. Too many teens have been led to believe that their agreement is a prerequisite to having to follow the guidelines we've given them. The confusion that follows is exhausting.

Nicole's mom came to see me looking for strategies in parenting her very popular daughter. "Nicole has already started pitching me about going to the legendary after-semi party in May. The most popular kids are having a boy/girl sleepover given at someone's house." Nicole is sixteen; her mom has a decision to make.

"She knows I don't approve of the boy/girl thing, which is why she's already started to give me all the 'rational' reasons why I should let her go. She's a good kid. I don't know, there is so much prestige involved with being asked, it's like I'm ruining her life if I say no."

Mom has a lot to consider: Is letting Nicole go to this party helping her become a healthy, responsible adult with values she can be proud of? At eighteen, Nicole will have to be able to handle a situation like this; at sixteen, does she have the maturity to handle the kind of decisions she might have to make?

As parents, once we've decided what to do, we let our teen know what our values are and how seriously we take our job. And then stop. Here's a synopsis of how the conversation between Nicole and her mom unfolded.

MOM: I've given this a great deal of thought because I know how important it is to you. In the end, it's my job to help you become a responsible, independent adult with values you can be proud of. This party is not in alignment with my values, so I'm sorry, but you will not be able to go.

NICOLE: But, Mom, how am I going to learn to be independent if you never let me do anything on my own?

MOM: Figuring out what level of independence you're ready for is my job. I'm sorry you don't like my decision. I love you and respect you, but when I go to bed tonight I have to know I did the best job I could.

NICOLE: If you *trusted* me you would let me go to the party. It's not like I'm going to do anything wrong.

MOM: I'm glad to hear you have confidence in your ability

to hold on to your values and I do trust you. But I will not put you in a situation that does not support my values. I'm sorry you're upset about this, but I am not going to change my mind.

THE END

This is the point where Mom needs to remember that Nicole is not supposed to agree. Often we explain and re-explain our decisions hoping our kids will finally see the light. This has just the opposite effect, confusing the teen and making them angrier. From their perspective, it's bad enough they're not getting what they want; they shouldn't have to act like they agree with us.

Remembering that our job is to launch them, we continuously assess their ability to handle independence, structure their opportunities to demonstrate responsibility, and do our best to stay connected. Parenting is an enormous job that takes time and support.

Sharing the Challenge

Parents often ask me if moms should talk to their daughters about sex and dads should talk to their sons. Yes. And moms should talk to their sons and dads should talk to their daughters. Having both parents talking gives kids a much fuller picture of human sexuality. Although kids will survive and even thrive with only one perspective, having two parents sharing the task of birthing a child into adulthood is a great advantage.

In my private practice, I've noticed that dads often have an advantage when it comes to being heard by teens. It could be that by the time a child reaches twelve or thirteen years old, the sheer volume of words that they have heard Mom speak has dulled their ability to take in much more. After twelve years, they know pretty much what Mom's going to say about everything. In many families, Dad still holds a bit of mystery. Dads simply have not worn out the child's ears with a steady stream of dos and don'ts.

Dads also have an advantage at this stage in their child's development because their presence is less infantilizing. To the teen, Mom's very existence can make them feel like a baby. Needing her for anything is terribly annoying. Even the smallest nurturing gesture from Mom is often met with a rebuff. Dad, however, often relates from a greater emotional distance, giving the teen the space he or she needs to actually hear what's being said. This is particularly true if the relationship between mother and child has been close.

Jamie, a sixteen-year-old, had been an anxious child who always enjoyed a close relationship with his mom. A late bloomer, his body had recently morphed into manhood. Overnight, being with his mom had become intolerable. "I don't know what has happened to her," he would complain in therapy, full of that itchy adolescent energy. "She is *always* talking to me, I can't even stand being in the same room with her." Mom, who had spent a great deal of her adult life helping Jamie negotiate his anxieties, was devastated at being so completely shut out. She also felt incapable of setting the speed traps and following through on the consequences that he suddenly seemed to need. She had never had to play that role before. Dad, used to being odd man out, was suddenly thrust into the primary parenting role. Initially skeptical about whether his wife would let him take the reins, with a little coaching, he was perfectly suited to the job. Jamie needed a strong man to structure his opportunities, deliver the consequences when rules were broken, and talk and/or show him the qualities that make a good man. Moms can have a hard time going through this. Jamie's mom shed a lot of tears. She said that emotionally she felt like she had years before, when she had weaned him, like she had lost her mooring, her purpose in the world. A few weeks after therapy ended, Jamie's mom called me. "You're not going to believe what just happened," she said. "Jamie just burst into the kitchen, grabbed a handful of cookies, and gave me a hug. He actually thanked me for the cookies! It's like he can see me again."

Once the appropriate distance had been established between them, Jamie was free to reconnect with his mom. Although the unusually dependent bond between Jamie and his mom intensified this transition, the same dynamic holds true, to a lesser degree, in many families.

At a time in a teen's life when he's struggling to figure out how to be a man, being with Mom makes him feel like a boy. What he needs is a dad who will tell him and show him the qualities it takes to become a good man, and that includes telling him how a good man directs his sexual energy.

Finally, Dad's a guy. Most kids have very few places where they can hear about life from a guy perspective. Most of their lives have been spent having their day-to-day reality fashioned by women. Both teen girls and boys can benefit from hearing about sexuality from a responsible male perspective.

Amy, always on the fringe of the popular group, entered high school with a vengeance. She had physically matured over the summer and was determined to put herself in the middle of the action. Unlike years past, she was now going to parties every weekend and there was a steady stream of boys coming to the house. I started seeing her when her parents found out she was bringing alcohol to parties and was hanging out with junior and senior boys. Young, immature, and enthralled with her newfound sexuality,

Amy had no discrimination about the kinds of attention she was getting. Any attention was good attention. At one point I asked her dad to join us in the session. I told him that it takes time and experience for a girl to figure out what boys are like and how to decide whether a boy is paying attention to her because he likes her or because he simply wants to see how far she will go sexually. I said that this was understandable because Amy was a girl and was therefore stuck in seeing things from a girl's perspective. I asked her dad to give her the guy perspective and to help her figure out how she could tell the difference between a guy who might really like her and a "player." Dad proceeded to name the different guys he'd seen coming to the house and one by one categorized them as potential boyfriends or players. Amy was stunned that he was pretty much able to nail each guy. Amy intuitively understood the distinction between these two types of guys, but she had never had anyone articulate it and put it into a context for her. I asked him to tell her why hanging with older guys was worrying him. He said that he remembered what he was like at seventeen. "I was a pig," he said bluntly. "I'm not saying every guy that age is a pig, but a lot of them are and they all spend a great deal of time thinking about how they can get a girl to have sex. You're a really pretty girl and you're smart, but you need more time before you're ready to deal with seventeen-year-olds." Amy alternated between being enthralled and appalled, but she heard *every* word.

Had this conversation been happening with Mom, there would have been ranting and raving about how Mom didn't understand and was ruining her life. With Dad, things stayed a lot calmer, in part because Amy knew that Dad was not going to be as emotion-ally drawn into the feelings of being a fourteen-year-old girl. At the same time, she was impressed with his perspective on boys. As totally "old" as he sounded, it also seemed like he knew something she needed to understand. Equally powerful, his concern felt like protection, whereas Mom's concern just felt like an intrusion.

I don't want to give the impression that teens are waiting to embrace Dad's involvement. They are teenagers, after all, and must act annoyed at any attempt to be parented. But they need Dad's involvement and are able to absorb it in an altogether different way than Mom's.

When Our Emotions Get in the Way

Teens aren't the only ones riding an emotional roller coaster. Parents can experience a real sense of loss as their children begin to distance themselves and go about the work of leaving. We miss the unconditional hugs, their desire to do things with us, the ease with which they once shared their feelings, and their unreserved interest in our opinions. We miss the child and how we felt being with that child.

I'm delighted to hear the giggles, the rapture, and "Oh, my God!"'s bubbling from my daughter when she talks on the phone. But five minutes later, when I ask her what happened in school, I get, "Nothing," and she suddenly looks too exhausted to even speak. "I've got SO much homework, I'm going to be up all night." And off she shuffles, head bent, shoulders crumbled, for all the world looking like she might not make it up the stairs. Sometimes I smile and remember how my mom always called me a drama queen. I stand back in amazement at the sheer energy it takes to make this transformation into adulthood. But sometimes, independent of all I know about this stuff, and all the psychological, developmental awareness that I can bring to these moments, I just feel sad. Two hours later, when she wants to cuddle before bed, I'm relieved and emotionally exhausted.

In my private practice and during my lectures, I see many caring, loving parents who have given their teens far too much freedom because they can't stand the drama and the pain of disconnection that happens when they say no. They allow themselves to be emotionally bullied by a child who is trying to negotiate the world without structure. No teen can be expected to want their parent to call ahead and find out if there is going to be adult supervision at a party or to have the maturity to know they are not mature enough to handle a boy/girl sleepover. More often than not they'll get angry with us and turn the precious few moments that we have into an argument. We can't expect them to be happy when we're doing our job.

Parents need support. We need to talk to our partners and friends. We need to reach out to extended family and, if family is not around, form parenting groups with other parents of teens. When we can talk about our feelings and concerns, and share stories and strategies with other parents, we are better equipped for those moments when we are at risk of sacrificing good parenting to maintain a connection with our teen.

• •

take it home

1. When was the last time you gave in to something your teen wanted to do because it seemed more important to stay connected? What price did he or she pay for that "connection"?

2. How many hours does your child spend digesting

some source of media? How could you structure his or her access in a way that would respect your child's independence and yet protect him or her from excessive stimulation?

3. Would you like your child to be popular? Why? How do you convey that?

● ●

The Gift of the Next Generation

During the thousands of hours I've spent listening to teens and parents, and certainly in dealing with my own teens, it often seems like some great cosmic joke that as we enter our teen years, when the opportunities for disaster peak, the last people that we want to go to for help are those who care for us the most. Perhaps adolescence is one of those phenomena that, from the perspective of the individual, makes no sense, but in terms of the species, has some sort of logic to it. Could it be that in some way the human race needs each generation to reject the generation before it? Could it be that we need teens to question everything, to see our hypocrisies, and irrationally plow ahead, as if they can do better? Is this ego-centered optimism useful somehow in giving the human race the shot in the arm we need *not* to stay stuck in the mess we're in? Perhaps in the grand scheme of things, there *is* a point to this madness. If not, at least it helps to think so.

I once watched a group of teens design a welcoming program for younger teens. The first thing they did was throw out everything they had ever seen done before. They didn't want a master of ceremonies or any kind of formal introductions. Everything they had seen adults do, they deemed inauthentic. I sat there wondering how they were ever going to get the job done if all they were focusing on was not doing what they had seen adults do. After a long while, they got to talking about what welcoming someone actually means. What were the qualities that made someone feel welcome? I watched as they discovered, for themselves, the meaning of welcoming. As amazed and relieved as I was to see the direction they were going in, I was dismayed at the time it was taking. Couldn't they have just asked me? I thought. I could have told them that plenty of people had gone through this before. But it wouldn't have been the same. Telling them wouldn't have mattered. To know it, to own it, they had to discover it themselves. That is the nature of our species. Taking ownership of the world, of their adulthood, of their sexuality, means owning the process of figuring it out for themselves.

The program they created was amazing. Each person was wholeheartedly welcomed in a way that captured the meaning they had discovered together. Nothing was predictable, canned, or inauthentic. It was a gift to sit there and learn from them.

seven

Preparing Kids for the Vulnerabilities of Adolescence

Inside the Head of the Adolescent

When a lobster becomes a teenager and reaches a size that makes its shell too confining, the shell cracks open and the lobster breaks free. But freedom doesn't mean much in the state it's in. For several weeks the lobster exists as this gelatinlike glob of very vulnerable flesh. Fortunately, a lobster is smart enough to know that as a floating blob of jelly it hasn't much chance of survival. Spotting a decent size rock, it hides itself until it grows a new layer of protection. No one expects the lobster to drive a car, say no to drugs, figure out what it means to be cool, or decide whether or not to have sex. The hormonal changes that human teenagers experience, in many ways, make them as vulnerable as teenage lobsters. We can support teens in making healthy sexual choices by helping them understand the specific vulnerabilities that come with the changes that are happening to their bodies, minds, and emotions. Teens can play an active role in strategizing how to best protect themselves from the risks that come with adolescence.

I've had the good fortune of teaching sexual health and responsibility to thousands of fifth-grade and middle school students. I always begin by diagramming the adolescent hormonal roller coaster on the blackboard. Pointing to the peaks and valleys, I act out the emotional extremes these hormonal shifts can create. Somewhere in the laughter and recognition that follows I ask, "How many of you have worried that you might be crazy?" Most raise their hands. Added to all the other anxieties that come with this age, most teens I meet are harboring a secret fear that maybe they're losing their minds. And why wouldn't they? On their best days they are a magnificent mess. At a time when the demands of parents, school, and peers are intensifying, everything they've always thought they could count on, their bodies, their brains, their emotional state, has become frighteningly unpredictable.

The face they wake up with looks different from the way it did the day before. Their noses have become oversized overnight, ears that never attracted any attention have suddenly taken over their entire head, skin erupts and clears without rhyme or reason. Their bodies alternate between feeling excitingly powerful and painfully vulnerable and, despite their most fervent prayers, will never look like those on TV. One minute life is awesome and they are filled with a crazy kind of energy, the next minute they are despondent and barely able to crawl out of bed. I sometimes think teens look in the mirror so often to simply remind themselves of who they are.

Making Sense Out of All This Change

A couple of months ago, a woman came up to me in the supermarket. She had recently attended my parent information night and her sixth-grade daughter was in my health class. "Dr. Maxwell, I just wanted you to know that when I asked Louisa what she learned in class she said, 'Don't worry, Mom. I get it, reproduction and the continuation of the species. It's all about controlling my sexual energy.' She was so matter-of-fact about it. I've always had such a hard time with this stuff. We started talking about things I never thought I could talk about."

I love moments like that. Louisa has a context for understanding the job ahead of her. And most important, Mom has a way of continuing the dialogue.

We start preparing teens for the chaos of adolescence by letting them know what the point of it all is. Puberty taught from the perspective of biology alone is just an embarrassing list of changes that happen to your body. Puberty explored as a way of understanding how you prepare for adulthood and independence is something worth paying attention to. It's easier to connect with teens when we're exploring the bigger context for why things work the way they do. The overriding quest is to find the value and meaning behind our actions.

The defining feature that separates a child from an adult is the ability to make more human beings. The context for all these conversations about puberty is recognizing that teens are in the process of growing bodies that are capable of reproduction. This doesn't mean that they're supposed to reproduce. Reproduction is a personal choice that involves many factors, not the least of which is a fully functioning adult brain capable of making that choice.

We continue by helping teens understand how their new experience of sexual desire is generating an energy inside of them. This energy makes them curious about everything sexy, causes their parents to look annoying, pushes them to check themselves out in the mirror every chance they can get, and is the reason they want to spend more time with their friends than their family. This is the same energy that will eventually propel them out of their home so that one day they can start a family of their own. Connecting the dots between feeling sexy and creating family is very important. Sexual energy is changing everything. The experience is powerful, wonderful, scary, and normal. When you're in the middle of it, while it's in the process of transforming your body and brain, things can get pretty stressful. It helps to be prepared.

Five Points of Change

The most defining feature in a teen's life is change. We can help teens visualize all the parts of themselves that are changing with a five-pointed star.

Each point on the star represents some aspect of a teen's life that is changing—body, brain, feelings, relationship with family, and relationship with friends. We start discussing these points of change with our preteens before they feel compelled to pretend they are not listening. We explore how each one of these changes makes them vulnerable, and we help them create a shield of protection—made up of strategies and resources that they can use to

who am i?
who decides?

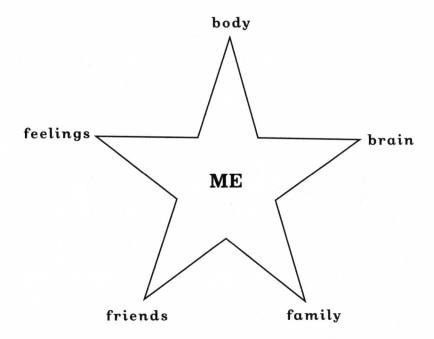

defend themselves until the tempest of adolescence has passed. Human teenagers cannot hide behind a rock until they reach maturity, but they can be better prepared.

The Body

It's easy to see the changes that are happening to the body. Most puberty curriculums and books about becoming a teen do a great job of describing these changes.[1] What we can add to these resources is how body changes make teens vulnerable. Watching TV with our teen is a good way of starting this conversation.

"It seems like advertisers know how vulnerable teenagers are about the changes that are happening to their bodies. It's almost like they design their ads to manipulate kids' vulnerabilities. What do you think?"

"Don't you think it's interesting that they pick gorgeous twenty-year-olds to play all the teens on this show and then try to sell you beauty products? That's a good way to make every teenager insecure."

Teens and preteens do not always have an easy time talking about how vulnerable they feel, but they are more willing to engage in a conversation about how someone is trying to manipulate them.

In health class, I ask them to design their own commercials. I ask them to think about the kinds of things that make them feel insecure and create an ad campaign that plays on those insecurities. You can see the lightbulbs go on as they experience how skillfully corporations manipulate their vulnerabilities and define what is beautiful, what is happiness, what is success. I've included below part of a conversation from one of these classes. The teens have just created a commercial for hair conditioner using strategies that play on teen vulnerabilities. I'm directing them to discover how they can best protect themselves from being manipulated by the media. I'm always so impressed with how sophisticated kids are when it comes to the media and how with a little prompting they can apply this sophistication to understanding their own feelings about themselves and the world around them.

teens talk about media manipulation

"Even when you know what they [advertisers] are doing, you still kind of believe it." Jillian's a waiflike sixth grader. She's just played the part of a popular girl in a commercial her team has created to sell hair conditioner.

"It's not that you really believe it's going to do all those things, if you use it, but it still makes you feel a certain way," says Mark, the director.

"We've got to add more music!" says Jamie, who's been responsible for production. "It's the music that makes you want to watch."

"They call that a subliminal message," says Grace, the intellectual in the group.

"Yeah, and we can sell the CD, too." That's Mark again, who will probably one day work for Warner Brothers.

"What can you do to protect yourself from manipulation?" I ask. "How can you prepare for all those feelings of insecurity?"

"It might help to not watch television," says Jillian.

"Yeah, like that's going to happen," says Jamie.

"I knew a kid once whose parents didn't let him have a TV," says Jillian.

"It's stupid not to have a TV; you don't have to buy all that stuff," says Jamie.

"You're still going to compare yourself to the people on TV," says Mark.

"What keeps you from feeling bad about yourself?" I ask.

"I think it's OK if you have friends that you can talk to," says Jillian.

"Friends, definitely," they pretty much all agree.

• •

As a parent of older teens, I would not expect to have a conversation like this. You might get nothing more than a grunt and a roll of the eyes. Try anyway. Your words do enter their brain and the seed is planted. The best protection teens have against a culture that feeds on their insecurities is a caring person to talk with, and parents who are willing to structure their time to reduce their exposure to stimulation that intensifies their insecurities (see Chapter 6).

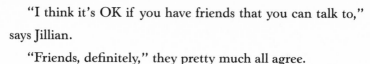

take it home

1. Watch television with your teen with an eye toward the commercials. Ask them if the commercial was effective. Did it cause them to want the product?

2. Ask them if they know any insecure kids who are always trying to fit in. Do they think commercials are more effective with insecure kids? Why?

3. If they were going to create a commercial, what specific teen insecurity would they target in order to sell the most products?

4. Listen a lot. Don't make it about them. Let the conversation meander where it will.

• •

Emotions

In many ways, girls are better prepared for the emotional upheavals of adolescence than boys. Unlike their brothers, who from an early age are discouraged from expressing emotion and encounter even more social pressure to ignore their feelings during puberty, girls are under no such restraint. In fact, girls are often directed to pay closer attention to their emotional state as a way of preparing for the hormonal changes that precede menstruation. The culture is rich with stories and advice, some good, some bad, about the emotional vulnerability women experience before their periods. Girls are advised to keep track of their cycle and be prepared for that time of the month when feelings can get intense. But in many ways, all of adolescence is one big premenstrual syndrome, for boys as well as girls. Hormones spike and crash willy-nilly, changing the body as well as the brain. There are biological reasons why suicide rates are so high in adolescence. Acknowledging the inner turbulence, understanding how it creates vulnerabilities, and proactively strategizing what to do when you feel like you're going to burst or crash is something we can start discussing with our teen at ten and eleven years old, before the storm begins.

The vulnerabilities that come with emotional turbulence may seem obvious, but they are worth discussing. Many kids begin to medicate themselves with an array of legal and illegal drugs to help them cope. Others escape by engaging in high risk or addictive behaviors. What other choices do they have?

What can you do when you're feeling really crazy? What do you do when you know you're not acting the way you want to, but you can't stop?

Some teens and preteens talk about going outdoors, someplace large enough to hold their excess energy. Some shoot hoops or walk the dog. Others choose the opposite and shut themselves up in their rooms, writing in their journals, or calling a friend. Some distract themselves with video games, TV, the Internet; others work out, play music, draw, or read a book. Some teens plug into their iPods and dance.

Just like adults, different kids have different strategies for dealing with powerful emotions; teens just have these feelings more often and with greater force. Sharing intensity-reducing strategies with our kids validates their feelings and gives them new things to try. We give kids an enormous life advantage when we teach them how to regularly check in with their physical and emotional state. Becoming aware of how they feel right now is the first step toward being in control of those feelings. Is their body tense? Does their head feel like it's going to pop? What are the signals, the physical sensations that let them know it's time to put protective strategies into play? If teens can acknowledge that a storm is upon them, they can activate a strategy before things get out of hand. When kids don't understand the fluctuating nature of their emotions, when they don't realize that there are things they can do to reduce the intensity, they are more likely to medicate themselves with drugs or alcohol.

• •

take it home

1. Discuss with your partner or friend what strategies you use to cope when your emotions become intense. What signals does your body give you that let you know you've reached your limit?

2. Discuss as a family what coping strategies people use to deal with emotional overload or stress. Ask each person to share their strategies.

3. Listen. There are no wrong answers.

4. Discuss if there are ways the family can support a person who is feeling very emotional or if they prefer to be left alone.

• •

The Changing Relationship with Friends and Family

The need for space, the need to separate from family, and the desire to be with friends is something teens feel but don't understand why. In the same way that parents benefit from understanding the dance of separation, teens are relieved to understand that there is a reason why their parents have become the last people on earth they want to be seen at the movies with. Teens like knowing that their parents are supposed to look so annoying, that this change in perspective is happening so that someday they will get fed up enough to leave home. But finding their parents annoying, as normal as it is, also makes them vulnerable. Most teens will tell you that their parents are their best resource when things get tough. What we can help teens understand is that adolescence brings an inner aversion toward accessing this resource. The most experienced and caring people in their lives suddenly become the last people they want to go to for advice.

The opinion of friends, on the other hand, ascends in importance to irrational proportions. I will often ask my students to rate, on a scale of one to ten, "importance of friends." It usually comes in at about eight or nine. I then ask them how they would have answered this question a few years ago. The number is significantly lower. Why is it that, as they get older, they value their peers so much more? The first and obvious answer is that friends are cooler, more fun, and understand them better. But as we begin to connect the dots with all the other changes that are happening to them, they begin to understand that replacing family with peers is all part of the process of leaving home.

Below is part of a conversation among fifth-grade students discussing how teenagers don't like to be with family and what that might have to do with peer pressure.

• •

teens talk about peer pressure

"I guess that's why my brother doesn't want to do stuff with me anymore," says Tony, whose brother is a junior in high school. This makes Tony an expert on all things "teen." "My whole family goes to Water Country, on the Fourth of July. It's a family tradition. But my brother doesn't want to go this year. He made plans with his friends instead. My parents are really mad."

"Can you think of how, when you put together friends-being-super-important and parents-looking-really-annoying, this can make your brother really vulnerable?" I ask.

Alice, thirteen, a leader in our discussion group, continues the theme. "My parents found out that my sister brought vodka to a party. You have to understand that my sister's perfect. She gets all As and everything. She told my parents she wasn't drinking, but she brought it because she promised her friends."

"My sister got caught smoking pot, but she won't even talk

to my parents about it, so they sent her to a shrink," Maddy, the quiet one, adds.

"If you can't talk to your parents because you're trying to separate from them and friends are the most important thing in your life, how does this make you vulnerable?" I ask again.

"My sister's doing stuff because she wants her friends to like her even more than she cares about what my parents think," says Alice.

"I think that's peer pressure," says Tony, "when your friends mean more than anything else."

• •

Conversations like this bring meaning to the overused concept we call peer pressure. Peer pressure is a natural vulnerability, one that serves a very important function for teens as they struggle to become part of the next generation. Teens are vulnerable to peer pressure because intensifying their relationship with peers is how they gather the strength to separate from family. This, combined with the fact that parents have become the last people they want to share things with, leaves teens dependent on peers for support and guidance. What strategies can they put into place to deal with this vulnerability?

Many kids talk about having friends from more than one group so that if they are rejected or pressured by one set of friends they have other friends they can count on. In class, we brainstorm about which other adults they can turn to for advice. Teachers, guidance counselors, coaches, ministers, priests, rabbis, and pediatricians are all mentioned. Lack of extended family, grandparents, aunts and uncles—as well as an often-marginal involvement in a religious organization—leaves many kids without resources outside of school. Teachers are left to pick up a great deal of slack in our culture and, when it comes to advising kids about issues related to sex, they are in a no-win situation: damned if they say anything that could upset the parent and overwhelmed by how much kids need to talk with someone. As parents, we must be very clear that we are a willing resource on any subject. We also need to let teens know that we understand that sometimes they will not want to talk with us, and that we will help them figure out who else they can go to.

• •

take it home

1. Who, other than you, could your teen go to for support? Brainstorm with your friend or partner a list of caring adults in your child's life. How could you strengthen those relationships?
2. The next time your teen chooses friends over you, let them know that you understand that this is part of growing up. Let them know that it might take you a little time to get used to this change.
3. Ask them to think about a time and activity that the two of you could do together.

• •

The Brain

Most puberty curriculums do an excellent job explaining how hormones affect the body. However, little or nothing is said about how they affect the mind. Why, at ten years old, would a kid never dream of getting in a car without putting on a seat belt but, at sixteen, he or she proceeds as if accidents and death cannot happen to them? How can we prepare adolescents for what's happening to their brains?

Only in recent years, through the use of MRIs, has science begun to understand the adolescent brain. As stunning and important as this information is, it's a stretch to try to make the bridge from MRI research to parenting advice. Still, understanding this information gives us a better appreciation of the challenges that teens face just trying to survive adolescence intact.[2]

Each of our individual brains is a great work in progress but none more so than an adolescent brain. Minute by minute, as their brains interact with the environment, they are literally creating their social/sexual/intellectual/spiritual identity. Every stimulus they encounter, every smell, taste, idea, and experience changes their brain. Every decision they make lays the foundation for the attitudes, habits, and perspective that they will bring to the next moment. What they become is the sum of all their momentary responses to the opportunities and challenges that the environment presents and how their brain, through neural connections, makes sense out of things. Understanding this rapidly evolving miracle we call the brain, gives us a new way of talking to our kids about adolescence and a greater appreciation of our job as parents.

You're Not Just Raising a Child, You're Growing a Brain

In the most simplistic and usable terms, the brain basically does three things:

- It creates new brain cells.
- It grows neural connections or pathways linking different parts of the brain.
- It prunes away the cells that are not being used.

Scientists used to believe that new brain cells were formed only in the first few years of life. After that, it was thought, we were pretty much stuck with what we had. But now we know that the brain also generates new cells in that precious and confusing time called puberty, with some continuation into young adulthood.[3] Most of this growth takes place in the frontal lobe, the most advanced area of the brain, in which higher level functioning, abstract reasoning, and decision making take place. Is it any wonder that our teens like to sleep as much as they do? It's not just their arms and legs and ears that are growing overnight, their brains are different when they wake up in the morning.

One would think that if adolescents have more brain cells in the part of the brain that is responsible for higher reasoning, we might see more of those higher reasoning skills. But brain cells alone don't amount to much. They need to be networked through neural pathways, and linked to all the other parts of the brain, in ways that give meaning to our experience. For example, a red convertible is just a red car without a top. But a red convertible that is linked by neural pathways to success, sexual virility, beautiful girls, and pulsating music has been given meaning and value.

I like to imagine the adolescent frontal lobes shimmering with new brain cells, like freshly fallen snow. How will these exquisitely human cells be used? What pathways will be formed? What will this particular brain spend its time pondering?

When we are faced with a new situation, our brain takes the stimulus—the sight, sound, touch, or taste—and tries to find something in our storehouse of memories to connect to it. A smell like apple strudel may link up with Nanny, happiness, Thanksgiving, and family. The sound of a passing train might link to good-byes and sadness or to freedom and independence. The neural links that connect our experience to our memories, thereby creating more memories, become who we are this moment and the basis from which we decide how to act in the next moment. Ever wonder why first experiences are so important? They lay down the first neural pathway, the ones that all other experiences then relate to. This is also why habits are so hard to break.

Habits are neural pathways that have been used so often they've become neural highways. In my brain, the link between Ben & Jerry's ice cream, TV, and "right before I go to bed" is a major highway. Every time I reinforce it, I make the habit harder to break. Every time I choose to do something different at night, I create a new pathway. It's hard work. When you find yourself standing at the refrigerator door without knowing how you got there, you're dealing with a neural link of interstate proportions. What an amazing thought to imagine the choices teens make today are creating the neural pathways that will direct their behavior throughout their adulthood.

Unused brain cells get pruned away. Much like a gardener who weeds the garden of things that aren't needed, the brain removes cells that do not appear useful. For example, language is easily acquired in the first three years of life, but this window of opportunity begins to close as parts of the brain specifically designed to learn language begin to be pruned away.[4] After that, language acquisition, although possible, is much more difficult. The teenage brain not only experiences an explosion of growth, it also begins to aggressively prune away what is not being used.[5]

As parents, we are the first gardeners of our children's brains.

They have been gifted to us to nurture, protect, and bring meaning. From the first time we respond to their cries, kiss their boo-boos, or help them with their homework, we are tending the garden of their amazing brains and helping to create pathways of compassion, enthusiasm for learning, and self-worth. What an overwhelming responsibility it is to tend the garden of the next generation of human brains. How crazy to think we can do it in our spare time.

A few years ago, I was preparing a workshop on drugs and alcohol and planned to use this metaphor of parents being the gardeners of their children's brains. I asked my son, who was fourteen at the time, what he thought.

"I like the metaphor, but I hate to tell you this, Mom. You are not the gardener of my brain," he said with no small amount of forced indulgence.

"What do you mean?" I replied. "I have always played a part in structuring where you go and what you see. I've shaped the amount of time you can do certain things and not let you do other things."

"You have always thought you were the gardener, but actually, Mom, I'm the gardener of my own brain. You can put me places and give me things, but I'm the one who has to use them. I'm the one who chooses. At best, you're the farm manager, but the gardener's job is mine."

I love teens. They hit the nail on the head and knock the pretentious wind out of my sails. They teach me so much, when I listen. Of course he is right. As a teen, he has become the gardener of his own brain. Moment by moment, he chooses which stimulus to attend to and which to ignore, which neural pathways to create, and which get pruned away. Does he listen to the teacher or flirt with the girl next to him? Does he attend to his homework or sit and space out? I may have managed to structure his time so that opportunities were available, but the moment-to-moment neural pathway–forming choices were his. In part, the pathways he forms and the habits he makes will depend on the genetic predispositions he was born with. But much will depend on his history of choices, the billions of neural highways that have been laid down since the day he was born. My ability to create opportunities to engage his brain has diminished with every passing hour from the moment he was born. If I'm lucky, I've helped him develop an appreciation for his brain and the skills to tend it well.

With the onset of adolescence, and the vulnerabilities that come with it, my job becomes much more complex. Gone are the days when I could control his environment. At a time when millions of new brain cells are forming in his frontal lobe awaiting opportunities for connection, I must manage the farm, monitoring the range of choices available to him and creating opportunities for experiences that, I pray, will form responsible and productive neural pathways.

Helping Them Establish a Relationship with Their Brain

The brain is such an amazing gift. We can start by showing teens what it looks like and how it changes over time. The National Institute of Mental Health has a Web site where you can see a healthy human brain as it develops and changes from age five to twenty.[6] Seeing something that you know is inside of you, working for you, intensifies one's sense of ownership and responsibility. Each young person should know that they have brand-new cells at their disposal that are working hard to connect with all the other parts of their brain. They should understand the opportunity that exists in each moment to lay down neural pathways that will serve and define them for the rest of their lives. Most of us think that the choices we make are simply momentary events that have nothing to do with our next choice. When you really comprehend that every choice lays a track in the brain that creates a tendency for the next choice, then what you choose to do or say *right now* becomes much more important. It's crucial not to use this perspective to push our kids relentlessly. *Sharing* information is different than banging someone over the head with it. I invite you to share this information with enthusiasm and wonder at the gift of being born a human being with all the possibilities that implies. The gardener's job is theirs.

Vulnerabilities of the Teen Brain

Ever wonder why your teen can't seem to plan ahead, makes a life-shattering catastrophe out of a small social slight, forgets that actions have consequences, and seems to think everyone is mad at him (even during those few moments when everyone is not)? These are just a few vulnerabilities that define the teen brain. When we acknowledge and discuss them with our adolescent, we help our children develop strategies for coping with the fluctuations of this magnificent work-in-progress called the teenage brain.

One thing we can help our teens to recognize is their tendency to overgeneralize. For example, thinking that they will never have any friends because no one sat with them at lunch is typical of teenagers—and of people suffering from depression. Much of the despair and hopelessness found in depression comes from not realizing that how you feel now is not how you will feel forever. A boy who has been rejected by his first real crush needs help to *not* interpret this rejection as a lifetime sentence as a "loser." Metaphors help. I often tell a teen who's sure that life will never improve that this time in his life is a chapter, a wretched chapter and hopefully a short one, but it's *not* the book. We can also give kids some advance warning. In my fifth- and sixth-grade classes, I explain how teens can get depressed because their brains make them believe that one small, bad thing will ruin their lives forever. We talk about how knowing these things can help prepare them for times they might need a "reality check" from people who care about them.

We know that teens, particularly when acting in a group of their peers, tend to forget to weigh their actions in light of the consequences.[7] When I ask fifth graders if they would ever get in a car with a driver who had been drinking, no one raises his or her hand. I tell them that a few years from now, probably when they are with their friends, they might get into a car driven by someone who has taken drugs or alcohol. We talk about how changes in their brain, combined with the excitement of being with their friends, will make them vulnerable to acting without thinking. If they are aware of this, they can be prepared for a time when it might be hard to think before they act. Knowing that your brain is making it difficult to think before you act and that your hormones are in high gear helps teens understand how hard it is to say no to sexual activity and motivates them to think through how they want to respond in sexual situations so they are prepared when the time comes. It's not enough to help kids understand the value of making healthy sexual choices; we have to help them devise strategies for working with a brain that is not always functioning at its best.

Research shows that teens may tend to misread people's emotions.[8] When asked to describe the emotion seen on the faces of people in a series of pictures, teens differed from adults in two ways. Adults used the front part of their brains, the higher-level, decision-making part, to make the assessment and were able to accurately describe emotions such as fear, shock, anger, and confusion. Teens used the more primal part of the brain designed for immediate response to danger. Not surprisingly, they often misread the emotions.

As a therapist and a mom, I probably hear a teen tell me that someone is angry at them twenty times a day. "My parents are always angry at me." "I can't work with that teacher because she's always angry." "My coach is impossible; he's angry at us all the time." "I can't talk with you when you're angry!" Now, this is not to say that teens do not experience a fair amount of anger coming at them during the course of a day. But I believe that a lot of the time they misread our frustration, confusion, anxiety, and surprise as anger. We would do well to tell them what we're feeling when we are feeling it, rather than assume that they are reading our emotions correctly.

How does this sound?

"I'm not angry at you. I'm frustrated that I don't know how to help you get your homework in on time."

"I'm not angry with you; I'm shocked that you waited until now to tell me you need a black skirt for chorus tomorrow."

"I'm not angry. I'm confused about how you could lose your winter coat and not realize it. How did you get home without freezing to death?"

OK. So maybe there *is* a little anger in there. But things would proceed better if we stated our more subtle emotions, for their sake as well as ours.

To make matters even more confusing to those of us who live with them, teens *think* they know everything, *look* as if they ought to be more mature, *act* insulted when we don't "trust" them, and do have moments when they actually *sound* absolutely sagelike. It can be hard to remember that our teens' ability to think things through in advance, and contemplate the consequences of their actions, is being challenged by the changes happening in the frontal lobe. Hopefully, understanding what's going on inside their brains adds a bit more compassion to our parenting.

It is not, however, a reason to give them a free pass. They still have to be held accountable for irresponsible behavior, or responsible behavior will never become part of their neural hardwiring. That said, we don't have to take it so personally. We don't have to berate, humiliate, or rage at them. We can understand that they still need us to structure their environment, eliminate excess stimulation, talk through simple strategies for tasks requiring long-range planning (while they're rolling their eyes), and repeat simple instructions over and over and over (without losing our sense of humor). Good luck!

••

take it home

1. Go into the National Institute of Mental Health Web site (http://www.nimh.nih.gov/science-news/ 2004/imaging-study-shows-brain-maturing.shtml) and look at the developing brain. Share this with your child and talk about how who he or she is becoming is always a work-in-progress.

2. When you're asking your child about their day, put the brain into the conversation. Ask them what neural pathways they paved today, what connections they made that they had never made before.

3. Think about how to make these conversations light-hearted and inspiring rather than anxious and lecturing. The brain is magnificent. Share your enthusiasm, don't make it a way to lecture and control.

● ●

When Everything Is Changing, Who Am I? Who Decides?

As important as it is to give our kids information about what's happening to their minds and bodies, and prepare them with strategies and resources to deal with the vulnerabilities of adolescence, there is still something missing. If everything is changing, and even your brain can't be trusted, how can you figure out what is the right thing to do? What part of you do you use to decide? In class, when I hand out the five-points-of-change star to each student, I ask them to put their name or the word "me" in the center of the star and then to think about what is true about them that does not change. I ask them to tell me what they are that is not their brain, body, emotions, or relationships with family and with friends. The discussion that follows leads us to perhaps the most significant part of talking to kids about sex. How do you decide how you're going to act as a sexual person? And what part of you does the deciding? Who is the "me" at the center of the star?

When I ask this question in health class, the kids go around trying to imagine what isn't their brain, body, or emotions. Eventually someone will say, "Do you mean like my conscience or something?" Another kid might ask if I mean his soul. Someone else will ask if I'm talking about the part of them that knows the difference between right and wrong. I'm always amazed at how energized kids get during these conversations. They are so eager to engage each other's wisdom to find ways of sorting through the endless choices they are presented with. Rather than labeling the center of the star a conscience or a soul, I ask them to imagine an experience that is available to them every day. I ask them to look in the mirror, looking past whether it's a bad hair day or at the latest zit that's popped out on their chin, and really stare into their own eyes. I ask them what happens when they look into their own eyes and ask, "Can I be proud of myself today?" Who is it that they're asking and who is it that knows the answer? That's the person at the center of the star. That's the person who, when they smile back at us, fills us with peace of mind. That's the person they will always be, no matter what is changing inside or outside of them.

Some kids will tell me that when they look in the mirror, they ask themselves if their parents would be proud of them. That's fine. Feeling that our parents would be proud of us is the first step toward developing the ability to be proud of ourselves.

Kids get this intuitively. We all do. Each of us knows the feeling of being proud of the goodness of ourselves. What we need is someone to help us remember how important it is to pause regularly, take a good look at ourselves, and ask the question.

This brings us to the most important aspect of sexuality, how we decide what to do, with whom, and when. What moral or ethical guidelines do we use? As parents, how do we help our children make choices that they can be proud of?

take it home

1. Have you prepared your teen for the hormonal lunacy that goes with this age?
2. Does he understand how his brain is operating differently, in ways that can make him feel crazy?
3. Can you remember a time in your own adolescence when you felt enormous energy surging through your body, feeling like nothing could hurt you?
4. Remember a song that got you juiced, driving at night with your friends? How do you feel when you see that energy in your teen? What messages do you give them about how to respect and direct that energy?

eight

· · · · · · · · · · · · · · · ·

Sexual Ethics and Religion: Finding Common Ground

In Holland, during the time of the Holocaust, a group of Christian parishioners went to their pastor and asked, "Father, what should we do about the Jews? If we take them into our home and hide them, we are risking our lives and the lives of our children. If we do not take them in, we know they face certain death." The minister looked at them with great compassion. "I cannot tell you what to do," he said. "My job is to remind you of who you are. Knowing that, you will know what to do."

When we talk to kids about being proud of the person who's looking back at them in the mirror, when we direct them to that person at the center of the star, the part of themselves that they can count on, that remains steady even when everything around them is changing, we are reminding them of who they really are.

As parents, the one thing we know for sure is that in the moment when our child is deciding whether or not to engage in sexual activity—whether it's kissing at a dance in middle school or intercourse in a college dorm—we won't be there. At that moment, whether they are being flooded with feelings of passion or simply wanting to find out what the big deal is, they will be the ones to decide whether or not to go for it and when or if to stop. How will they decide? What principles of ethical behavior will they use? Have we prepared them for the feelings they will have? How does a responsible person decide when to be intimate with someone and when not to? Like the pastor, we cannot make that choice for them but we can help them recognize who they are. We can acknowledge the complexity and confusion of becoming a sexual person, we can let them know our values, and we can point them to that part of themselves that longs to be proud.

Looking for Opportunities to Find Common Ground

Since I began talking and writing about teen sexual behavior in 1998, I've had the great, good fortune of being able to present my work in public and private school systems, parent organizations, and conservative and liberal religious settings of various Christian and Jewish denominations. This diversity has given me a unique perspective on how as a culture we have come to divide sex education into different parts, with each part taught in a different domain of the child's life. Schools, religious institutions, the media, and, most of all, parents each contribute to a child's understanding of sexuality. But, more often than not, no one is pulling all the pieces together in a way that makes sense. One part that too often falls through the cracks is teaching the child what constitutes ethical sexual behavior. How does a responsible man or woman choose when and with whom to engage in sexual activity?

When I hand out the star (see page 111) to a parent group, school, or in another secular setting, I have the participants put their name at the center of the star. We talk about helping our kids develop a relationship with that part of themselves that can be proud of their behavior. We discuss how to raise children who not only understand the right thing, but choose to do it even when it is not the easy thing.

When I'm working in a Christian community, the participants put their name and a cross at the center of the star and, together with the pastor, we discuss how being a Christian provides a constant reminder of that sacred part of them that never changes. In a Jewish community, we put a six-pointed star at the center of the five-pointed star and the rabbi discusses how the part of them that never changes is their relationship with themselves as Jews.

In every environment, we can examine how feeling good because you did the right thing feels different than feeling good because you got something you wanted. Treating someone with respect feels different than taking what you want from them. We can explore different ways of talking with our teens about the feeling of pride that comes from knowing you've done the right thing. We can also talk to our teens about looking in the mirror when it's difficult to face the person looking back at you because you do not feel proud of yourself, and how every day gives you a new opportunity to be proud once again.

Why Teaching Ethical Sexual Behavior Often Falls Through the Cracks

The same principals of decency that guide us in all of our behaviors apply to sexual behavior. Yet we often address, or fail to address, sexual behavior as if sex existed in an altogether separate realm from the rest of human behavior. School curriculums in middle school and high school address issues like bullying and drug abuse by teaching skills that support respect for others and for ourselves, yet ignore ways in which these same skills can be applied to teaching ethical sexual behavior. Teachers and administrators witness daily the damaging and risky sexual behaviors our kids are engaging in and the effect these behaviors are having on teen's self-respect and ability to function as students. But they are frustrated in their attempts to address the issue. As one teacher put it:

"There have been many times that I can see a kid dressing and acting in a way that I know is setting them up for a fall. I used to try and say something, you know, in a supportive way to help them see what they're heading into. But now I see it as way too dangerous. One time I told a student that they were not dressed appropriately for my classroom. I mean we have a dress code here, but try applying it. This time I did and I got a call from the parent, raking me over the coals. Why did I pick on *their* kid? The sex thing can get crazy here sometimes, but who wants to stick their neck out?"

Rather than trying to find the common ground between parents, religious perspectives, and education, we often retreat to our separate camps, accusing each other of not doing the job, virtually abandoning our kids to learn what they need from TV. When the producers of the PBS documentary "The Lost Children of Rockdale County"[1] (see page 11) returned two years later to see if the indiscriminant sexual activity among young teens had diminished, they found little had changed. Despite the intensity of public outcry and the involvement of school, parents, and religious organizations, no common ground for teaching kids ethical standards of behavior had been found.

All parents share the frustrations of trying to raise good people in a culture that often is at odds with our values. We all face the anxiety that comes from realizing that as our children reach adolescence our time of telling them what to do is swiftly coming to an end. With each passing day we realize that we will not be there when they are making the decisions that will define them. If we can keep ourselves from becoming politically polarized into warring camps in the "culture war," it is possible to find common moral ground. It is possible to share the common goal of helping our kids develop a strong sense of who they are, by giving them an ethical framework from which to make responsible sexual decisions.

What's God Got to Do with It?

What role does religion play in educating children about how to ethically handle their sexuality? For some families a great deal, for others not at all. Many families pick and choose which religious guidelines fit the understanding of sexuality they want to pass on to their kids.

Several years ago I received a call from a rabbi asking me to speak about ethical sexual behavior to parents and preteens who were preparing for their bar and bat mitzvah (a Jewish rite of passage from child to adulthood). I was thrilled. A religious setting felt like the perfect place to discuss ethical behavior. And what better time to address sex than in preparing for a ritual that initiates one into a community of adults! How much easier it would be to talk about ethical sexual behavior when all the participants shared the same religious tradition. An added benefit was that this was a natural community that could follow up on my presentation by providing teens with a safety net of responsible adults who could set standards for behavior. I asked the rabbi to join me in the presentation so that we could connect my way of talking about sex with his expertise on the traditional Jewish understanding of sexuality.

The presentation was a great success, and since then I've done the same work with priests, ministers, and rabbis, ranging from very conservative to very liberal. These collaborations have provided me with a treasure trove of wisdom and information about human sexuality that I have incorporated into the values that I pass on to my own children.

When I started speaking in churches and synagogues, I found that more often than not the participants were surprised that they had been invited to discuss sex in a religious setting. I began to hand out questionnaires asking the teens and their parents what their religion has to say about sexual behavior. Typical teen responses were:

"Nothing, religion is about God, not about sex."

"Religion just tells you not to do it until you're married."

"I don't know but I don't think we should be talking about that stuff here."

Parents were equally confused. One parent wrote: "I almost didn't come today because all I remember as a teenager is being given a bunch of dos and don'ts that made no sense to me. But now that I'm a parent and see what's going on, I need to figure out what to say to my daughter. I'm hoping this will help."

What could become meaningful conversation about the role of sexuality in our lives is often reduced to a simplistic list of don'ts presented in a context of guilt and embarrassment. There is often little, if any, attempt to communicate the meaning and value of sex in a manner that validates the power of sexual desire or makes sexual guidelines relevant to the day-to-day experience of teens. Parents who regurgitate these guidelines are often viewed as being hypocritical.

Ellen is a sixteen-year-old high school junior. She's been going with her boyfriend since their freshman year and they've been talking about becoming more sexually intimate. Raised in a religious family, she does not see her parents as a source of guidance and is angry about how her mom uses religion.

"She's always telling me not to let Ted pressure me. I don't know; I guess it's easier for her not to think I might want to have sex. But then she's always checking up on me like she's thinking I'm having sex all the time or something."

"Have you ever thought about just talking to her about where you're at with all this stuff?" I ask. "It could be she understands more than you think."

"Really bad idea," says Ellen. "Any time sex comes up in any way, she starts telling me what the Bible says and it's like she's just saying that stuff because she thinks she's supposed to be a good mother or something. OK, so I'm sixteen now and maybe that's too young. But I know for a fact that when I'm in college and, like, if I'm still a virgin, she would definitely think there was something wrong with me. Everyone thinks there's something wrong with my cousin."

"Maybe your mom's clear about what she thinks about you having sex now but really isn't sure how she feels about it when you get older."

"Well, then she shouldn't have to use the Bible. Why doesn't she just say so?"

Teens want to engage us in meaningful conversations about how and when to be sexual with someone. They can tell when we don't believe, or maybe even understand, why the guidelines we give them make sense.

Many of the religious guidelines for sexual behavior were written at a time in human history when children came into their sexual energy and moved directly from their parents' home to the marital bed. There was no extended adolescence; no prolonged single status. Understanding how to handle one's sexuality responsibly when you move directly from your parents' house to starting your own family is very different than figuring out what you have to know today as a single, working person navigating a sexually saturated environment for ten to fifteen years. So what do different religious guidelines, written at a time so unlike our own, have to offer our understanding of sexuality?

For those who believe that religious teachings are divinely inspired, that is enough to give them validity throughout time. But it is overly optimistic to think your teen will necessarily agree with you. Our children have been raised in a country where arguing and debating is applauded as a way of finding the truth. They are living in a culture that celebrates sex for the purpose of pleasure. If you think differently, it is *your* job, and that of the religious community to which you belong, to make the teachings relevant by being willing to engage in meaningful dialogue. To do that, we need to educate ourselves as to why our faith holds the values that it does. What is the deeper understanding of sex that these guidelines are based on? All of us are more willing to follow a rule if we understand the principles that give it meaning. Be willing to be challenged or understand that your teen may well be nodding in agreement and acting very differently.

Looking Deeper at a Valuable Resource

Whether or not religious considerations inform our understanding of sexual behavior, there is a great deal to be learned from how religion values the role of sex in our lives. It is religion, after

all, that perhaps holds humanity's most in-depth recorded understanding of what sexuality means to us as human beings. Science
is acquiring more and more information with regard to sex,[2] yet it
is still in its infancy when it comes to understanding the complexities of human sexuality. At its best, science can give us important
information, but it cannot give meaning or value. At this time,
our best collective understanding of sexuality is found in our art,
philosophy, and spiritual texts.

In this chapter I've chosen to share some of the insights I've
gained from working with leaders from different spiritual traditions because they have greatly enriched my understanding of
sexuality as well as informed my parenting. This is by no means
an in-depth look at the vast amount that religion has to say on the
subject of sex, and my experience is limited to the Judeo-Christian
traditions. Other spiritual traditions also have a great deal to add
to our understanding of how human beings understand sexuality.
The two perspectives I've included below shifted my own point
of view and gave me a richer way of addressing sexual behavior.
They helped me find my own personal language for talking with
teens about the value of sex (see next chapter) that stands as an al-
ternative to our current consumer-driven version of sex for power
and personal gratification. It is this level of understanding that our
children, and perhaps all of us, are hungry for.

Two Beautiful Ways to Talk About
the Meaning and Value of Sexuality

One evening I found myself standing with a rabbi in a synagogue,
talking about sex with a group of about two hundred Jewish high
school students. We were going back and forth discussing is-

sues of sexual ethics and taking questions from the teens. At one point, the rabbi was explaining that how they choose to conduct themselves sexually was ultimately up to them, that there was no doctrine that forbade sexual expression, but that the fundamental principles of being a good person that they had been learning since birth applied to sex as well, and that sex was not to be viewed as a commodity to be acquired but was an act of profound intimacy.

One very brave young woman in the audience raised her hand and asked, "How will I know when the relationship I'm in is important enough to start thinking about having sex?"

Wow, I thought. This is really hitting the nail on the head. How, indeed, do any of us know?

What the rabbi said next was sheer brilliance. (I paraphrase.) "There is a Hebrew word in the Bible that means 'to know'; the word is *da'at*. This word is often translated to mean sexual intercourse, as in Adam 'knew' Eve. Sometimes we make jokes about this and say things like, 'Did you know her in the biblical sense?' meaning did he have intercourse with her? But this is not the full meaning of *da'at*. It does not just mean sexual intercourse. It means knowing in the most profound way that a person can know another, knowing on the level of the soul. This kind of knowing is like revealing oneself, completely revealing all of who you are and having the other completely reveal himself or herself to you. This word implies a level of knowing that necessitates love and trust. It is not an accident that the word also means 'intercourse.' In our sacred texts, there is no distinction between intercourse and this level of knowing.

"So if you are contemplating sexual intercourse and you are a Jew, you might first ask yourself, Do I know this person at that profound a level? Have I revealed myself to him or her completely?

Have they truly revealed themselves to me? But before you even ask yourself that question, ask yourself this: Do I know *myself* well enough to know what I have to share with someone else? You are all in your teens. This is the time to figure out who you are. Who is this person at the center of the star? Know this person first before you consider knowing another. And now, Dr. Maxwell is going to talk to you about the person at the center of the star. That's the person you've got to get to know before you think about having sex."

I just stood there, breathless. In two minutes, he had put into words what I had struggled as a mother and a therapist to find the words for. And to think it was all hidden in that ancient word, *da'at*.

This way of discussing how to decide whether or not to have sex did not lay down a law that a teen would feel compelled to argue with or prove wrong. It gave criteria for how to think about making a decision about having sex that was based on becoming aware of your self first and then assessing the quality of your relationship. It opened up the possibility of dialogue and personal investigation. It made you want to think more about it. It gave new importance to taking time to figure out who this person is who lives at the center of the star and how knowing this person informs our decisions and infuses our lives with meaning and value. And finally it uplifted the conversation and made me grateful for the generations of wisdom that have gone before us.

That next spring, I was standing with a minister speaking to a group of Christian parents. He was reciting a passage from the Song of Solomon, a love poem exalting the feelings of a young bride gazing upon her naked husband. He was quoting the Bible and people were blushing.

"Sexual intimacy is the most intense experience of pleasure known to man. It is supposed to be so," he said. "It is a mirror, a reflection of the intimacy of the Godhead. When a husband and wife share their intimacy, it is a taste on earth, however brief, of the joys of heaven and the result is the creation of a living, eternal being. Every culture has sexual urges," he continued, "there must be a corresponding gratification. That thirst and its gratification come from God. This is one of His gifts. But the body and soul cannot be separated. Sexual union unites, within the individual, one's body and soul. *Bodily vulnerability without soul vulnerability reduces your humanity. Sexual activity without the involvement of the soul will consume you.*"

Now this last part, about sexual intercourse being the unity of body and soul, sounded a lot like the rabbi talking about the word *da'at*. That way of knowing also united the body and soul as each person revealed fully their physical and spiritual self to the other. Both traditions agreed that sexual intercourse outside of that level of body/soul unity, or "knowing," reduced one's humanity.

There were also differences in how these two spiritual leaders spoke about sex that were relevant to the congregations to whom they were speaking. These differences, with regard to sex, can be found between different denominations that use the same spiritual texts. But to my ears, there was so much more that was similar. I couldn't help thinking about how hungry my students and clients are for conversation about meaning and value. Not just in the domain of sex, they are craving meaning at all levels of being a conscious human being in the world. Both the Jewish and Christian traditions brought meaning to the sex act. Both warned of a life less richly lived if we ignore the part of us that longs to connect both our body and that which gives value to our experience. Call it a conscience, call it a soul, call it the person at the center of the star. What's important is that we begin this discussion with our kids.

Preparing to Become an Adult

Every invitation I have ever received to speak in a religious setting has happened because parents requested it. These parents are not just looking for a new way to keep their kids from having sex, they're trying to find words to help their kids see sex as something more than momentary gratification or a way to become popular. They may or may not agree with everything their religious tradition says about sex, but they're hoping it will give them a richer understanding from which to address the subject.

Every religion has a rite of passage into adulthood where the young teen is given an in-depth, extended series of instructions about what it means to be a responsible adult in their religious community. These instructions end with a celebratory ritual (bar mitzvah, confirmation) where the teen is initiated into the adult community. What better time and place to teach them how to ethically and responsibly direct their budding adult sexual energy?

It is the ability to reproduce that separates children from adults. To initiate teens into the adult community without addressing how that community understands the roles of sexuality in our lives doesn't make sense. Many teens receive guidance about handling their sexuality as part of their religious training. I invite parents to become part of that learning and to really look at what is being taught. Find out how your teen is making sense out of the instruction and become a resource so that you can help them understand what they are learning and how they can use this information in their day-to-day lives.

take it home

1. What does your religious tradition have to say about the meaning and value of sexuality? Is there more that you can learn about that?
2. If you have no religious affiliation, can you imagine that there might be something to be learned about sex from exploring different religious perspectives?
3. What ethical framework has your child been given about how to handle their sexuality by either educators or spiritual leaders?
4. Have you been included as an important participant in their education?
5. How can you become involved in their spiritual/sexual education?

....

nine

Developing Guidelines for Sexual Behavior That Reflect Your Values

Whether or not we believe that sex is a divine act or that religion has any role in defining what constitutes moral sexual behavior, we are still left with the job of giving our kids a way of thinking about sex that is both responsible and ethical. But what do we really believe? What are our values when it comes to sexual behavior? When our children reach the point in their development when they are wondering whether or not to release their sexual energy with another person, what guidelines do you hope they will use? Should they be in love? Is it important to respect the other person? And what degree of sexual expression is OK? Will these guidelines change as they get older?

As complex and confusing as it may be to address these questions, most of us have a pretty good idea of what responsible sexual behavior is not. So let's start there. Forcing someone to have sex is not responsible. Having unprotected sex is not responsible. Deciding to have sex when you're less than fully conscious is not responsible. Pretending you like someone in order to have sex is not responsible or ethical. If we do nothing else as parents, we should at least give our children these minimal rules of safety and decency because even these are not reflected in our culture.

Below is a list of eleven principles I hold with regard to sex. They reflect the meaning I give to sexuality. These principles have been formulated by my own personal history, my education, and the time I've spent listening to teens, parents, educators, and spiritual leaders. But most important, they reflect the values I want my teens to understand as they begin to formulate their own standards of behavior. These principles will not necessarily be similar to yours, and that's a good thing. Use them as a jumping-off point for figuring out your own truth about sexuality.

• •

eleven principles for sexual behavior

1. Your body, and the decision about how to use it, belongs only to you. Anyone who tries to force or manipulate you into having sex of any kind does not respect himself or herself, and does not respect you.

2. How you choose to use your body and how you choose not to use your body becomes part of who you are. The choices you make today tell you and the rest of the world what you're about and, more important, how you see yourself physically, emotionally, and spiritually.

3. Any kind of sexual behavior that involves another person is an expression of intimacy. The more sexual you choose to be with someone, the more you are choosing to share who you really are.

4. Being sexual with someone can be fun and playful, but it is always personal and private. Sex is never a spectator sport.

5. Choosing to express your sexuality is a conscious act. Allowing it to "just happen" or engaging in sex when you are less than fully conscious is dangerous and diminishes your ability to give it the consideration it deserves.

6. Letting someone know your body and exploring someone else's body is an amazing experience. It should only be done with someone you respect and trust. Sex should never be used to gain power, popularity, or as a cure for loneliness.

7. Before you let anyone know your body, make sure they have shown you that they care enough to want to really know you.

8. Before you invite someone to really know you in an intimate way, spend time getting to know yourself. As you better understand who you are, what you believe in, and what you care about, you begin to be ready to share yourself with someone else.

9. Never pretend to care about someone as a way to get him or her to be sexual with you.

10. Being sexual with someone should feel good. It should never be painful, disgusting, or humiliating.

11. Sex is always a two-way street. If the person you're with only cares about their own pleasure, they don't really care about you.

• •

. . . .

take it home

1. Read these guidelines with a friend or partner and talk about them. What here is true for you? What is not?

2. Copy this list of things to think about (see Appendix 4) and give it to your teen. Tell him or her that you want to hear their ideas, and then schedule a time to discuss at some later date.

3. When discussing with your teen, ask them if they think these principles are too idealistic or perhaps too vague. Ask them if they know of situations where these guidelines might have helped someone make a better decision.

4. Ask them if they've ever felt pressured to do something sexually that they were not comfortable with.

5. Try to LISTEN more than you talk. The goal is to start an ongoing dialogue. Let them know you understand how complicated this all is and that nobody has all the answers. If appropriate, share some of your confusion at their age but DETAILS ARE NEVER WELCOME.

. . . .

Is Sex an Expression of Intimacy?

We live in a time when we can no longer assume that our children think that sex is an expression of intimacy. As discussed in Chapter 1, "friends with benefits," "booty call," and "hooking up" are all expressions of a trend toward regarding sex as solely an expression of personal pleasure. At face value, when we think about our twelve-year-old, this trend seems appalling, but as we begin to reflect on all of the different kinds of relationships one can have over a lifetime that include some level of sexual expression, it becomes harder to figure out what kind of guidance to give our children. Should sex always involve some degree of personal intimacy? What quality of relationship is necessary for sex to be OK? And even if we figure this out with regard to sexual intercourse, what about all those other types of sexual expression? What quality of relationship justifies kissing? Oral sex? Do we have to love the person? Like the person? Or is mutual respect and honesty all that is necessary to maintain our personal integrity?

Am I Supposed to Be in Love?
From Sacred to the Booty Call

There is no way to define what level of sexual expression is appropriate to what quality of relationship at any given point in our child's development. There's a reason that we tend to throw up our hands and hope for the best. That said, as we struggle to find our own principles of ethical sexual behavior it helps to think about how we feel about the relationship of sex to intimacy. We can start by thinking about what kind of relationship we would hope our child is in before they consider having sexual intercourse.

One contribution that a spiritual perspective can add to our understanding of sex is that it sets the bar when it comes to conceptualizing sex as an act of profound importance, with certain religions defining sexual union as a divine act sanctified by God and a commitment for life. Think about it. Something that we are biologically driven to do with our bodies is so important, so profound; so divine an act that we can only do it if we are willing to make a lifetime commitment. Do we believe this?

It's not hard to understand why sexual intercourse is connected to the divine. One doesn't have to have any religious beliefs to experience sexual intercourse as a profound act. Even with all our scientific understanding of procreation, the fact we can have sex with another human being and create a third human being still has the ability to fill us with wonder and change the very foundation of how we see ourselves and our job as human beings.

But in a day and age when one can have sex without even considering procreation, when we can separate sex from conception at will, do we still hold the value that sex must always be a divine spiritual act?

Whether we want our children to think that sex always has to reach this bar is a question that as parents we have to be willing to address. And what about all those other kinds of sex? If they can't result in making babies, does that mean they don't count as divine? If we don't think that a lifelong commitment is necessary, what do we believe? Should we only have sex in the context of love? Is it an act of intimacy and caring? Is mutual pleasure OK? Do our guidelines for what sex should be change with the age of the person considering sex? We all want our twelve-year-olds to be virgins. What about our twenty-four-year-olds? Are there different expectations for boys than for girls? Are there exceptions? Is there a time in your life when you're supposed to experiment? Where on the continuum of sexual expression, beginning with "spiritually sanctified by marriage" to "booty calls," do you stand? Our kids are going to land somewhere on this continuum. We can help them become more conscious of their decision if we talk about it with them first.

sexuality continuum

Sex as a spiritual act sanctified by God and a lifetime commitment

Sex as a spiritual act in the context of a loving relationship

Sex for pleasure in the context of mutual caring and intimacy

Sex by mutual consent but for your pleasure only

Sex as an expression of personal power or prestige without regard for another

This continuum of sexual behavior is meant to make you think about what sex means to you. It can also be used to start a conversation with your teen about what sex means to them. What is ideal? What is realistic? What reflects your values?

take it home

1. Use the sexuality continuum as a way of reviewing your own sexual history. What has your sexual experience taught you about the relationship between sex and intimacy?
2. Discuss what you've learned with a friend or partner, NOT WITH YOUR KIDS.
3. What do you wish you had known?

4. Would you pick a different place on this continuum for your daughter than for your son? How do you support that?

5. How can you talk to your kids about what you learned without going into inappropriate details? Practice with a friend.

6. Ask your child what he or she thinks about this continuum of sexual expression.

7. LISTEN A LOT.

8. Share your thoughts.

• •

Let's Talk About Love

Many teens are trying to identify at what point in a relationship they should consider becoming more intimate and, despite the trend toward sex without intimacy, many believe that love should be a prerequisite to sexual intercourse. In the anonymous questionnaires I hand out to teens and parents, I always ask the question "When do you think it's OK to have sex with someone?" One of the most common answers is "When you're in love." But what exactly do they mean by "in love"?

I began to include the question "How do you know that you love someone or that someone loves you?" The most common answer among teens I've worked with is "You just know, it's a feeling that you have." These answers gave me pause. They started me thinking how I had never talked to my children about love. What is love? How do you know that someone loves you? How do you know that you love someone? Isn't it amazing that a concept of such deep significance to us, understanding this feeling we call "love," rarely enters into our conversation with teens?

Why Aren't We Talking About Love?

Maybe we don't take teenage love seriously. Yet when you consider the risks they may be taking in the name of love, how can we not talk to them about it? Do we assume that understanding love is something that you just pick up along the way? That if we have loved them enough or modeled love in our relationship with our partner, they will just know what love is? Of course, loving our kids and our partner lays a foundation for understanding love, but it's not enough. Teens are trying to figure out the feelings they're having. They're wondering how they will know if the person they like really likes them back, and at what point those feelings will be transformed into that magical thing called love. If we believe that sex is more than a commodity to be acquired, if we want our kids to use their teen years to explore what it means to be in relationship with someone rather than just satisfy their desires, we might start by figuring out how to talk to them about love.

A cherished teacher once told me that love is the most powerful force in the universe and that understanding love is a lifetime journey. Perhaps we start the journey by attempting to define what love is not. What kinds of feelings do we confuse with love? If we could just help our kids sort out the kinds of feelings that love isn't, they might begin at a better place on the road to understanding what love is.

There's a Difference Between a Loving Feeling and a Lusty/Sexy Feeling

Having teenagers can trigger memories we have long forgotten. Eons ago, I was returning from a day at the beach with my boyfriend. It was a perfect day: the songs on the radio, the wind blowing through the car, his arm around me gently moving his hand up and down my shoulder. I don't know what it was but, at that moment, I had my first true experience of sexual desire. The word "swoon" comes to mind. It had never happened before. It's not that we hadn't kissed or made out, we had and it had been fun, but I had never felt like this. When we got to my house, he walked me to my door and kissed me good-bye. I thought I was going to faint. I can remember clearly walking into the house, shutting the door, and sinking to the floor. What was happening? I had never experienced anything like this before. I remember searching for a way of understanding what was happening, and then it came to me. This must be love. It wasn't.

I tell this story in workshops for mothers who are looking for positive ways of helping their daughters through puberty.

"Do you remember when you first found out that having a lustful feeling for someone is not the same as being in love?" I ask.

I'll never forget one mom who answered, "About a year and a half after I got married."

Imagine how wonderful it would be if we could clarify just this one point for our children. Sexy feelings are not the same as loving feelings. Sometimes they go together and that's really great, but just because you have one does not mean that you have the other. Although boys and girls both can get confused about this, I find that girls particularly confuse lust and love. Boys tend to know from the first time that they get a spontaneous erection from just seeing something sexy that lust does not signify love. Girls, whose sexual stimulation depends on a wider range of factors, are more likely to think that anything as powerful as that swooning feeling must mean something profound.

Teen boys and men whom I've worked with often confuse love with a feeling of ownership. They interpret "love" as the feeling that a girl is exclusively theirs. If they feel jealous thinking about her being with someone else, this is seen as confirmation of the validity of their feelings. This immature understanding of love can quickly lead to a crippling degree of mutual dependency. I sometimes ask boys, "Just because she only wants to be with you, how do you know this is love? Maybe she's just really, really needy?"

I've seen girls and boys equally confuse love with rescuing someone or being the sole provider of someone's urgent needs. There seems to be a need to nurture in many girls that is misinterpreted as love, as well as a feeling of importance at being the one chosen to relieve his needs, whether physical or emotional. But what makes the topic of love so difficult is that all of the above feelings might have something to do with love.

Providing for another's needs, nurturing each other, making a commitment to our relationships are all elements of what it means to love someone, but without experience or understanding, they can be turned into dependency, manipulation, and disillusionment.

We will never be able to fully define love for our children. We will never be able to spare them a broken heart. Many of us will look for love in our lives and probably find what we are capable of receiving. What we can do is engage our teens in conversation. Let them know that wanting to give and receive love is an amazing human adventure and worth every moment of confusion and embarrassment. Let's talk with them about how mystifying love can be and how often we can confuse it with dependency, jealousy, and feelings of physical desire. Perhaps the best we can do is get them thinking about what love really means and take comfort in imagining how much better prepared they will be to know love when they find it.

●●

take it home

1. What have you learned about what love is not? Discuss this with your partner or friend.
2. Movies and television shows provide many opportunities to discuss love. When watching with your teen, find the moment to ask, "Do you think he loves her?" "How can you tell?" "Do you think she loves him or just needs him?"
3. Keep it light. You're planting ideas, not giving a lecture. Listen and remember you can bring it up again another day.

●●●

....

ten

Forming One's Sexual Identity Online: Parenting Just Got a Lot Harder

CooRay934: wuzup

   AndTwo: nuttin rly u

CooRay934: my m bein a total BTCH

   AndTwo: so u do j

CooRay934: OMG who sed that

   AndTwo: dan said j told sam

CooRay934: sM or sT

   And Two: st

CooRay934: st's f'n liar

   AndTwo: omg u r SOOO too pissed

CooRay934: st's pissed bc she wantd to hook up w j

   AndTwo: lol

CooRay934: ask her

   AndTwo: u wanna?

CooRay934: omg y and more than that ho bri

   AndTwo: DAM

Sarah's mom was devastated that her thirteen-year-old daughter would talk about wanting to have sex online and refer to her mother and friends as bitches and whores. When she confronted Sarah about this IM exchange, Sarah responded with a mix of attitude and outrage at her mother's lack of respect for her privacy. "It's not like we're actually doing any of those things," Sarah said. "It's just the way everybody talks online."

But in my office a few weeks later, things seemed more serious. Sarah's friends Brianna and Christine had stopped sitting with her at lunch. Christine had e-mailed Sarah saying they weren't into "hanging out with hos." Without knowing why, and without having planned it, Sarah—always on the fringes of the A group—had finally delivered on the content of one of the e-mails by giving a senior boy a blow job at a party. She didn't know why she had done it. Sarah said she had taken some vodka from her parents' cabinet to the party and that she had been the first to take a drink that night. She insisted that the alcohol had had no real effect on her decision to have oral sex. She had just "felt like it" and thought it would be fun to tell her friends. Given that her "friends" were now using her behavior as a way to exclude her, Sarah was left feeling hurt and confused. She knew for a fact that Christine had hooked up (in this case meaning oral sex) with two different guys that year, which was somehow OK, but Sarah's hookup had made her a ho. Sarah was unable to process why or how it was that she had decided to engage in oral sex. She seemed emotionally disconnected from the event. Instead, she was obsessed with finding new ways of getting back into the good graces of the alpha girls.

All thirteen-year-olds are not engaging in oral sex, but they are all in the developmental process of creating their social/sexual identity. Who are they? How do they fit? Are they attractive?

Will others find them attractive? When preparing for school in the morning, Sarah, like thousands of her peers, stands in front of the mirror trying on different looks, different attitudes, different responses, imagining one social scenario after another and practicing how she will respond. By creating, discarding, and re-creating her look, she is in the process of forming her social/sexual identity. The lunchroom is where she will test it out. Will she be brave enough to sit with this one, talk, flirt, or even make eye contact with that one? Bravado, attitude, style, boredom, and sexual teasing are all tools in the game of finding out who you are as a sexual being. The problem is that, now, kids are doing this online, outside the domain of any adult guidance.

Where's the Lunchroom Monitor?

Do you remember the school cafeteria? A sterile place with wretched food where friendships are created, played with, and destroyed; where teens try on and discard social identities as quickly as they discard their lunches. How you look, whom you sit with, who talks with you and who doesn't is all part of an elaborate process of figuring out who you are by where you fit in the social hierarchy of your peers. Do you remember the lunchroom monitor? Often she was a bedraggled teacher, serving her time, whose job was meant to keep things within the bounds of decency.

The Internet has become the new "virtual lunchroom." But unlike a real lunchroom where one has some accountability for one's language and behavior, the virtual lunchroom has no social constraints. Language, threats, teasing, and rumors can be pushed beyond what anyone would dream of doing in person. Thoughts, feelings, and attitudes are sent in an instant, no one can see you,

you don't use your real name, you speak in code, and adults have no idea what you're saying. It's the Wild West of social/sexual identity building. Anything goes. There is no beleaguered adult holding down the chaos and there are no rules of decency.

Click Into the New Adolescence

Stop right now. Put down this book. Get on your computer and access buddypic.com. Welcome to the new lunchroom. What awaits you is thousands of pictures of teens and preteens all hoping to be ranked on a scale of one to ten by their peers. A high ranking on buddypic.com is priceless in the hierarchy of cool. How do you get a good score? By being as sexually provocative as possible. Look further. Read the profiles of these kids. They are exploring who they are by how they project themselves into this virtual world. Are these kids as tough, sexy, and worldly as they are pretending to be online? Probably not. A virtual world, where there is no accountability, is a perfect place to play at being something you're not quite sure you want to be.

But there are consequences. As the sexual envelope gets pushed, some kids, usually those on the fringes, the wannabes who only belong minute by minute at the whim of the popular kids, feel pressured to perform, thus raising the ante for everyone and subtly shifting the sexual norm one instant message at a time.

Sarah doesn't know why she decided to give Justin a blow job. It "just happened." Would it have happened without the Internet? Maybe. But the Internet, in conjunction with the intense corporate pursuit of young teen dollars, has speeded up the whole social/sexual process.

Now look at myspace.com and then facebook.com. Roam

around. Observe the subtleties of the social interaction. Watch how messages reflect who likes whom and who is being dumped. See how kids project their identities, gather friends, and negotiate intimacy.

Log onto livejournal.com. This is one of the hundreds of online journal sites where a great many teens write about the angst of adolescence and click it off into cyberspace, hoping they can be known, somehow, by someone, even as they struggle to know themselves.

For Shy Kids, Socializing Online Is a Mixed Bag

"It's just a way of keeping track of things, you know, like how I'm feeling. I don't know, maybe somebody is getting it. Lots of people have written stuff back. Sometimes it's garbage, but mostly it's cool. Sometimes I know who it is because I can tell by what they're saying. But sometimes people try messing with you. I don't care. I mostly do it for me."

Jasmine is a fifteen-year-old freshman. She's immature for her age, has one equally immature friend in school, and has never gone out with a boy. She brings in some of her journal entries to therapy as a way of sharing how lonely and cut off she feels from the excitement she imagines other kids her age are having. Posting her thoughts and feelings in an online journal has given her a way to connect without the insecurities that come from interacting in person. Ten years ago she would have kept a diary. The thoughts and feelings expressed in the diary would have been a way of working out her loneliness and social fears. Now she seems to be working through them online. Aside from the obvious hazards inherent in sharing one's thoughts with strangers (see Appendix 2),

I am concerned that her need to connect with other kids her age, experiment with her look and style, make mistakes, be hurt, and try again are all experiences that she is less likely to have because she is spending so much "social" time online. How real are the connections she's making? Is this a great venue for a shy girl who needs to test the waters online before she feels ready to engage in the real world, or will the Internet become a crutch that allows her never to risk venturing out of her comfort zone? Fortunately for Jasmine, she welcomes the opportunity to explore her strengths and insecurities in a therapeutic relationship. She wants to sort out her feelings. She's willing to challenge herself in small steps that over time will give her a sense of social competency. But many shy kids become overly dependent on the Internet, and fail to develop the social/sexual skills that they long for.

I started seeing John during his first year of college. Like Jasmine, he had been shy and withdrawn in high school. He had a few male friends who shared his enthusiasm for gaming online, but he had never come close to having a relationship with a girl. During his second semester of college, a girl had come up to him at a party and offered to hook up (in this case, "hook up" meant having sexual intercourse). A few minutes later, feeling incredibly lucky and scared, he found himself in the bathroom with the girl, unable to sustain an erection. When this happened a second time, in a more intimate setting, he started therapy. John's entire social/sexual life had consisted of online conversations, superficial flirtations at parties after a lot of drinking, and an addiction to online pornography. From the time he was twelve years old, he had masturbated almost daily to online porn sites. He says that seeing pictures of girls is more stimulating than actually touching a girl and he's afraid that he might not be able to have an orgasm in any other way. The Internet had given John some sense of social connection. Easy access to online porn had become his only expression of sexuality.

Online Porn

One of the Internet issues that parents are most concerned about is online pornography. How do they keep their children from seeing it? What effect will it have on their sexuality? Is it really any different than our generation reading *Playboy* or *Penthouse*? Yes. Online porn comes to you. It pops up on your screen whether you are looking for it or not. For a child, this makes pornography seem like something everybody knows about, which for many children means it's something that needs to be explored.

Jake is the youngest of three boys. At ten years old, he wants very much to belong to the cooler world of his teenage brothers.

"I had a feeling something was up," said his mom. "When I had my husband check the online history for Internet use on our home computer, we found that Jake has been searching out pornography for the last two months. He's been going on almost every day. He's started to develop physically much earlier that his brothers, but we never imagined he was interested in any of this stuff. The sites he's been looking at are really graphic and hard core. I know he feels ashamed that we caught him. I don't want him to think sex is bad, but I have to somehow help him understand why pornography is not the right way to understand sex."

In the same way that I was concerned that my son's first exposure to naked ladies was connected to violence, Jake's mom is concerned that Jake's first understanding of sex is linked to the images he has seen online. How will this effect his social/sexual development? How does early access to pornography inform his understanding of what it means to be a man? Just as we are beginning to measure the effect on our daughters of being "sexualized" before their time,[1] we might begin to examine how as a culture we are "sexualizing" our sons, its effect on their understanding of intimacy, and their awareness of themselves as men.

Lost and Confused in Cyberspace

We will never fully understand how the Internet is changing our culture, our children, and ourselves. Like television, radio, and the telephone, the Internet is just becoming part of who we are.

But there is a great deal that we need to know about the Internet. We need to understand how our children are speeding up their developmental process in a virtual world with no adult supervision. We need to understand the role this tool plays in acculturating our children. We need to do our homework and find out about all those aspects of the Internet that our children know about but we don't even realize are out there. We have to find a way to show our children that our values are relevant in this new virtual world.

Several years ago, I worked for an agency that serviced teenagers from immigrant families. These teens understood American culture and were more fluent in English than their parents. They were also less inclined to listen to their parents' advice or follow their parents' rules.

Cut off from their new culture, immigrant parents have difficulty connecting with the network of adults, such as coaches, teachers, and neighbors, who could assist them in providing a safety net of guidance for the teen. Instead, they are often dependent on their children to tell them what is going on. Immigrant parents often put few or no restrictions on the kind or amount of media their children access. Rather, media and technology often represent all that they want their children to have.

But this unlimited access to media further disconnected the teens from their traditional family values. What these teens understood as funny, attractive, important, and successful drifted further and further from their parents' understanding. These differences reached critical mass in adolescence. With the advent of hormones, as the tumultuous process of separation began, the power and authority the parents needed to keep their teens safe and to hold them accountable for their behavior had been lost. These immigrant parents had lost their ability to guide their children into adulthood. Because they were intimidated by the enormity of what they didn't know about the language, technology, and culture and were isolated from other adults, they had relinquished a huge piece of acculturation to the media. The hierarchy of the family structure and the natural lines of authority and respect were broken.

One does not have to be an immigrant parent to feel the same sense of powerlessness. When it comes to the Internet, we are all in a foreign country. How many of you knew about online journals or buddypic.com? Most of us do not understand this way of communicating or even know how to do it. We too are isolated from other parents. When our children were younger, we met at birthday parties and teacher conferences. Now we rely on our children to tell us what's going on. Like immigrant parents, we admire our children's competency and feel proud to give them access to such amazing tools as the Internet, cell phones, and text messaging. But many of us have handed over huge parts of our job as the teachers of family values and ethics to the media. We've given our offspring the keys to a new world which they've entered without us.

The Front Door Never Belongs in Your Child's Bedroom

I imagine the Internet creating an invisible tunnel from my house to the entire world, like the rabbit hole in *Alice in Wonderland*. The computer screen is the portal through which our children have access to everything the world has to offer: information, knowledge, inspiration, new people and places, and desires of every shape and form. We cannot even begin to imagine how this unlimited access will change our world and ourselves. Through this portal, our kids can invite anything into our home, *anything*. And in the click of a button they can disappear through it. If your computer really were a portal to another universe, wouldn't you want to put that portal in a place where you could keep an eye on it? Wouldn't you want to know if a stranger had entered your home or if your child had decided to click into another dimension in space?

Guard the Portal

Always have the computer in a place where you can see it.

This is a good rule of thumb for any source of information, but it's particularly true of the Internet. Just as it would be unsafe to have your front door open into your child's bedroom, don't put the portal-to-the-universe there, either. Now this can get hairy with laptops. As convenient as they are, especially for older teens, think long and hard before you invest in a portable portal, and if you do, plan on how you are going to limit access to the Internet to public places only.

There are other ways to guard the portal. You can invest in blocks that limit your child's access. Unfortunately, these blocks are often too restrictive and not restrictive enough. They can block access to harmless sites that have a restricted word in them (like "sex") and allow access to undesirable sites that have been intentionally designed to outwit the blocks. Research blocks, install them if they fit your situation, and don't fool yourself into thinking you have done enough.

There are ways of finding out where your child goes online and ways of recording their e-mails and IMs so that you can read them at a later time. In some situations this is a necessity. But it is not optimal. Needing to rely on outside restrictions means you have not taught your children internal restrictions. This takes time. You have to know your child and set up a structure firm enough to protect him and flexible enough to respond to his growth and maturity. For example, blocking your twelve-year-old's access to pornography is just common sense. But without teaching him how pornography can become addictive and what your values are with regard to pornography, you have not prepared him to live successfully with his sexual energy in the twenty-first century.

Making Our Values Real in the Cyberworld

Like immigrant parents, we need to help our children understand that our values transcend cultural trends and the latest technology. The principals of ethical behavior relate to every aspect of their lives, even the Internet. We start by looking more closely at how we use the Internet as a tool for communication, gathering information, and accessing stimulation.

Teach Kids the Value of Their Words

For a teen, the most important thing about the Internet is that it is a way of giving and receiving communication. Teens define their social/sexual identity through interactions with their peers, and those interactions need guidelines. We parents might not have figured out how to IM someone, but we do know what constitutes responsible communication. We know that the words you use reflect who you are and what you're about. Since our children were born, we have been teaching them the principles of responsible communication. How we speak to our children, and how we allow them to speak to us and others, has always been part of our parenting. The Internet forces us to articulate what we mean by responsible communication and how that translates to online conversations. Like immigrant parents, we need to think through and communicate to our children how to carry our values and ethics into this new world.

There are many ways of talking online. Whether you're IMing, leaving an away message, entering a chat room, sending an e-mail, or posting an entry in an online journal, you are making a statement about who you are. Teens love to push the envelope, play at being different people, and take on different attitudes. Often, this can mean exploring different ways of expressing their sexuality. As parents, we can acknowledge the excitement our kids feel talking to their friends online and help them understand the need for limits. Responsible communication involves taking another's feelings into account, telling the truth, and valuing the importance of words. Here are some guidelines; add to them, change them, and make them your own:

- Do not use words in any form to harm or threaten another. Threatening someone online is against the law.
- Do not start or spread gossip.
- Never use words to intimidate or bully.
- Do not use curse words or obscene language.
- Be careful about "fooling around." Never say that you will do something that you really do not want to do.

High school and middle school are times of high drama, when words are frequently used to assert power over another, often with damaging results. The Internet gives us a good reason to sit down with our kids and talk about our values and define our expectations for ethical communication. We can let them know we understand how hard it is to uphold these standards, especially online, and can help them remember by posting our guidelines on the computer (see Appendix 2).

Teach Our Children to Protect Themselves from Excess Stimulation

Sometimes, more is just too much. All of us, but most especially developing teens, are fascinated by the unlimited stimulation that the Internet delivers. Whether it's online poker, Duke Nukem, or one more hand of Spider Solitaire, we are all susceptible to wasting precious hours online. Learning how to protect ourselves from too much stimulation is critical to our physical, mental, and spiritual well-being. Deciding when more is simply too much is a matter of priorities and values. Just as the immigrant family must decide how to access the American culture in a manner that preserves the family's core values, the Internet must be approached from a core set of principles that help children decide what is worth their time and what wastes it.

Culturally speaking, we are always slow to see the pitfalls of having too much of anything. It takes a national obesity epidemic to get us thinking about whether more is always better. Excessive sexual stimulation at an early age can alter social/sexual development. There is another book to be written about how our children are drowning in excess stimulation. It is enough here to just warn parents that the Internet provides an endless torrent of stimulation and we are just beginning to understand how cripplingly addictive some of that stimulation can be. In the same way we teach our children the importance of controlling and directing the energy of their desires, we can teach them to pay attention to the amount of stimulation they are accessing online and help them find a healthy balance. One approach is to record how we spend our time and see if it matches our values.

• •

take it home

Have each family member track what they do all day for three days. For example, record how many minutes you spend sleeping, eating, grooming, driving, and shopping; doing chores or homework; going to school and/or work; watching TV, being plugged into the Internet; spending time outdoors or engaging in an activity with your family (see Appendix 3). Have each family member average the time spent on each activity during those three days and record it on a pie chart. Then sit down as a family and compare charts. Look at your child's average day and see if it reflects a life that supports physical, mental, emotional, and spiritual health. How much time is he or she passively accessing an electronic source of stimulation? How much of your child's brain development is happening through interaction with sources outside of your awareness? How much time does he or she have with you without any electronic stimulation? How at risk is she for falling through the "rabbit hole"?

● ●

Teach Children to Assess the Value of the Online Information

We are drowning in information. Unlike much of the world, we have no trouble accessing tons of information on anything and everything. Back when most of us were teenagers, doing a research paper meant getting to the library, figuring out the Dewey decimal system, hoping the library had what you needed, and feeling lucky to find three or four good sources. The skill set we learned was how to *access* information. No more. Recently, when my son searched for information on an obscure tribe of indigenous people in Colombia, he found more than two hundred journal articles and papers in fifteen minutes. And these were just the materials written in English. The problem was that we didn't know how to tell which information was credible and which was not.

Some of this accessibility is truly remarkable. It is astounding to think that anyone can access course material from the Massachusetts Institute of Technology. That fact alone almost balances the relentless Viagra ads that keep popping up on our computer screens. Unlike for people in China or Saudi Arabia, for us getting information is not the problem. Figuring out whether the information is reliable and what it means is the skill set we need to develop now. Who knows if the *Journal of Sexual Addictions* published in Sydney, Australia, is a valid source of information? How would you find out? Life is busy, so we tend to grab information that supports what we want to believe and move on. At a time when bloggers influence public policy, how can we help our children figure out what to believe and what to pass over? Assessing the *quality* of information on the Internet and understanding what that information means is the challenge of the twenty-first century.

Although that topic lies outside the scope of this book, as parents, we must persist in finding ways to help our children evaluate the information they get online.[2] In the cyberworld, fiction can be packaged as fact and sexual predators can appear to be "friends." The more we can learn about the Internet, the better prepared we are to teach our kids to protect themselves from being manipulated or even victimized.[3]

Teaching Children the Value of Community, Family, and Friends

It amazes me how fast marketers have caught on to the passion teens have for friendship and a sense of belonging. You can have hundreds of "friends" online. You can create social networks on your cell phone. The power of connections online is real, but what is it doing to our understanding of the word "friend"? How is this online world substituting for our lack of community and extended family? How can we teach our children about community and friendship when our own social network is so often dismantled?

Oprah's Great, but Where's the Neighborhood?

Which brings us to Oprah. I love Oprah. I turn on *The Oprah Winfrey Show* and it's like a family friend has just come over for a cup of tea. But the truth is, I am sitting alone in my kitchen. How is it that Oprah has become our best friend and source of family wisdom? How did we get so isolated from one another that we are relying on Oprah, Dr. Phil, or a book like this one for information about parenting? One of the most difficult challenges of parenting teens today is our isolation from other parents of teens. The cultural network that supported our parenting when they were young—parent conferences, sideline conversations with coaches or scout masters (often fellow parents), religious instruction teachers, and the endless round of birthday parties where we compared notes and assessed fellow parents—is gone. As our kids enter middle school, teachers are much harder to contact, coaches are too busy, religious instruction often trails off when puberty begins, and parties are off-limits to us. How are we supposed to know what's going on? How do we know who the troubled kids are, who the irresponsible parents are, which teachers and coaches empower kids and which run them down?

Of course we don't need the same level of involvement as we did when they were younger. But how can we responsibly parent our children when our ability to know what's going on in their lives, when the social network of caring adults with whom we shared information and upheld standards of behavior unravels so dramatically in middle school? Teens and preteens don't congregate in neighborhoods that can reinforce a sense of community and interpersonal responsibility. They hang out in malls designed to stimulate their desire, and promote the value that self-worth comes from having more stuff. Nowadays, teens faced with little access to extended family don't have the opportunity to use an aunt or grandfather as a sounding board when parents become "too annoying." The insight, advice, or compassionate ear of a caring aunt or grandmother has been replaced by the relationship advisors on the Internet or afternoon television programming for kids. Churches and synagogues are often no longer the center of community life; and with them go many of the gathering places for teens as well as the social pressure imposed by the community to hold parents responsible, not just for their children, but for all our children.

Without the network of caring, nonparent adults, TV characters often act as replacements. Teens talk about the lives of the TV characters and celebrities they track every week with a greater sense of dependency and affection than they do their own families. And where are we? Ironically, the caring, responsible, loving adults in their lives are working as hard as we can to keep all that technology available to our children. Mothers and fathers—the core reality makers, the time structurers, and consequence deliverers—are not at home. Hanging out together after school is part of how teens develop their social/sexual identity. Hanging out after school with access to alcohol, cable TV, and no adult to set expectations for behavior is leaving their sexual development to the merchants of cool.[4]

Make Connections Wherever You Can

Whenever I speak to groups of parents, I urge them to look around the room and acknowledge that right here is the social network of caring adults that our children need to navigate adolescence successfully. We can give our kids a sense of community by connecting with each other, forming parenting groups, meeting weekly at a local coffee shop, organizing a family nature walk, or joining an organization with other families that supports meaningful community work. It also keeps us on top of what's really happening in their world.

We know "everyone" isn't doing what our teens tell us everyone is doing, but we don't really have any social network that can tell us what really *is* going on. And God forbid you try to connect with or contact parents of your children's friends, or even ask the most basic question about parental supervision at a party. You will be treated as if you were betraying the very fabric of your relationship with your child. They would rather die a thousand deaths than think that you're contacting anyone they know or who knows someone they know. Do it anyway. One of the best outcomes from my parenting seminars, particularly those I do in religious settings, is to establish a way for parents of teens to stay in touch with each other. Some of these groups have been meeting regularly for years. Out of this ongoing parent-to-parent contact comes the potential to hold one another and our religious and academic institutions accountable for providing the structure and moral guidelines our children need.

Ironically, some parents form online parent groups. They use the Internet to establish relationships with other parents of teens, often around a particular concern such as drug involvement. They share information and draw strength in the wisdom and experiences of other parents. If this works for you, great. Certainly it is a useful way to get practical information about the Internet and to help our children use this tool safely. But it isn't community. We need to talk with aunts and uncles, grandparents and cousins, rabbis and ministers, and priests and imams. Our kids need adults in their lives who know them and know their families, and who will hold them accountable.

Start Talking Now

Independent of all the bells, whistles, and rush of excitement that comes with any new technology, the principles of healthy, responsible living remain the same—but they can seem much harder to focus on.

There is something compelling about clicking that mouse. Aligning our Internet use with a healthy, balanced lifestyle—remembering to remain conscious of how much time it is taking out of our lives—is an important skill to teach our children. We can remind ourselves that the most important part of growing up is not acquiring more information or figuring out how to access more stimulation. The most important part is understanding who we are, why we're here, what kinds of experiences bring meaning to our lives, and what is a waste of time. Right now we can take the time to assess our daily schedule and imagine what a balanced family life would look like. We can teach our children how to decide when they are being manipulated by this technology, and when they risk losing huge chunks of precious family time pursuing pleasures that only lead to wanting more. We can refuse to make the mistakes of our immigrant ancestors and remember that our love and experience give us exactly what we need to guide our children, no matter how much new technology muddies the water.

take it home

1. Look up buddypic.com. How are Web sites like this affecting kids' sexual identity? Tell one other parent about this site and start a discussion.

2. Ask your teens whether or not they have a profile in an online journal (facebook.com, myspace.com, etc.). If they do, tell them you want to take a look.

3. How are you making sure the Internet is being used in a way that aligns with your family values?

eleven

....

Where Are We Going?
Musings on the Twisted
Road to "Sexual Liberation"

We Are All Reinventing Our
Relationship to Sexuality

Inevitably, when I talk with parents and teachers about teen sexuality, someone asks, "Why do you think things have changed so dramatically? How did we get here?" Although most of my energy as a mother and psychologist is spent finding the words to help teens make healthy decisions, I think that addressing how it has come to pass that our children understand sex so differently than we do, particularly the way teens are separating sex from intimacy, is worth thinking about. Looking back at how I thought about sex when I was a teen, remembering the questions that I wanted someone to answer, and thinking about the social context that pushed me into making the decisions I made, has helped me find the words to talk with my own children and understand the pressures they feel.

Throughout this book we have looked at how culture influences sexuality. We've examined the impact of the media, the Internet, and the lack of both community and extended family on our children's developing sexuality. This chapter presents a series of snapshots past and present that captures some of the questions and dilemmas our children are facing today. I offer them as a way of exploring your own thoughts about how sex has changed since you were a teen and where we might be going. There are questions at the end of every section. Use them as a way of examining your feelings and values. With the support of your partner or friends, examine your own personal experiences, remembering the questions you had as a teen and young adult, the advice you were given, and the advice you wish someone had given you.

If you choose to discuss these questions with your teen, refrain from recounting details of your sexual past. For parents who have experienced sexual abuse in their childhood, I urge you to consider counseling before you begin to address sex with your child.

If Boys Don't Do It, They're Gay; If Girls Do It, They're Sluts. Who Has the Right to Say Yes? Who Has the Responsibility to Say No?

Each generation seems destined to push the sexual envelope further than the generation before. Standards of sexual behavior evolve generation to generation as adolescence, with its hormonal surge, interacts with the cultural factors specific to that moment of time. Today we are watching the hormonal surge of our adolescents colliding with the new technology of the Internet (see Chapter 10). During the sixties, we experienced the baby boomers' huge collective sexual energy interacting with a culture that was for the first time sending a great many of its young men and women off to spend four years together in a mostly unsupervised environment, while delighting in the new Pill, which freed men and women from unwanted pregnancy. Is it any surprise that this collision gave birth to the "free love" movement? Perhaps free sex would have been closer to the truth. Living through this time as a teenager, I remember trying to understand the feelings my body was experiencing, the inconsistencies about sex that I saw all around me, and all the while sensing that something important was changing.

Flashback: 1969

Place: On the Road Back from Visiting Colleges with My Dad

A late bloomer, about to enter college, I was thinking a great deal about sex and decided to use this time alone with my dad to ask him what he thought about sex before marriage. I valued my dad's opinion because he approached things logically, a "put all the information on the table and come up with the best solution" kind of guy. I'll never forget his reply.

"If you have sex before you get married—" I could tell he was weighing each word carefully. "No man will ever marry you."

"Why?" I asked.

I was prepared for "men want virgins," which seemed to me based on some sort of biological argument about being able to prove which kid belongs to you or some male ego thing about needing to think you were the only person that your wife ever found attractive. Both arguments seemed lame and I was ready for a debate. What I got was a surprise.

"Because men want to have sex all the time. The reason they

get married is so that they can have a steady sex partner. If you have sex with a man before you get married, there is no reason for him to marry you."

Wow! Nothing I'd experienced or read about had prepared me for that line of reasoning. But then again, what did I know about men?

"Is that why you married Mom?" Nothing like reality to unravel an illogical argument, I thought.

As parents, we should always be prepared for the question that ties the guidelines we are giving to our own behavior. Teens so enjoy uncovering the BS. This is the great gift and curse of having teens.

"No," he replied. "But that had a lot to do with it. Men can't help themselves. That's just the way they are."

What was he saying? Men are these crazed animals that sniff their way through the universe desperately seek out a receptacle for their overwhelming passion? What about my sexual feelings? I knew I had them, but I also knew they had never reached any level of intensity that would make me want to marry someone so that I could do it all the time. Were men's sexual feelings bigger than mine?

"Do you think that men's sexual needs are greater than women's?" I asked.

"Absolutely," he answered. "No question. And once you're in the world you'll realize that's true." The ultimate parent fallback: "I'm more experienced. I win."

I was silent for a long time. What did this mean? I didn't think he was right about the sexual desire thing, but there was no way to prove it. He was a man after all. I couldn't ever know what his feelings were. But he also couldn't know mine.

I remembered coming home one day from high school. My mother and a few friends were sitting at the kitchen table drinking wine and reading *Cosmo*. They were having quite a time of it, giggling like schoolgirls. They started whispering when they saw me. Later I found out they'd been reading an article about woman's sexual pleasure, specifically clitoral orgasms. None of them had ever heard of a clitoris before. Neither had I, but if what *Cosmo* said was true, it seemed like something worth exploring.

Back in the car, I was wondering if it was possible that my mother, raised in a very religious family, had grown up believing only men had sexual desire. Maybe she didn't think it was OK for her to have sexual feelings. One thing I did know was that I didn't want anyone marrying me so that they could have a steady sex partner. Yuck! Aside from the blatant lack of romance, love, and respect, it just seemed like my end of that deal would leave a lot to be desired.

"Well," I began, "I think I'm going to have to have sex before I get married."

I could see the skin on my father's temples begin to move back and forth. Not a good sign.

"Why is that?" he asked.

"Well, if it's true what you say about men only wanting to marry you because they need a steady sex partner, I'm going to have to make sure that I find someone who isn't marrying me for that reason. The only way I can make sure that happens is by having sex with him first. If he still wants to marry me, I'll know it's because he loves me, not because he just needs someone to have sex with."

My poor dad, what a car ride we had!

If I hadn't been going off to college, if the birth control pill hadn't been available to me, this conversation would not have happened. I was never the kid who was going to act out sexually. I just wanted to understand the feelings I was having and figure out what to do with those feelings, particularly now that I was leaving home and would have the opportunity to have sex. There were a lot of questions to be answered:

Are men's sexual desires stronger than women's?

My limited experience told me this might be true.

Do girls have the same right to explore their desires as boys do?

Even during this time of "make love not war," girls who "made love" as indiscriminately as boys were ostracized. Maybe there was something wrong with them.

Time: 2007

Place: Having Tea with a Friend

I told this story recently to a friend. Her response astounded me. "Your dad was right," she said. "That's why women are having such a hard time getting married today. Do you know how many women are in long-term relationships where the man will not commit to marriage?"

Is this true?

Are women, restricted by the demands of their biological clock, destined to have to use sex as a tool to get men to marry them? Was Doris Day right?

Time: 1940s & 50s

Place: The Movies

Theme: If Sexuality Were a Pie Made Up of Desire and Responsibility, Boys Would Get Desire and Girls Would Get What's Left

If we look at the movies from the 1940s and 1950s, particularly the romantic comedies with actors like Frank Sinatra, Dean Martin, Doris Day, and Rock Hudson, it's amazing to see how comfortable we were with the idea that men have uncontrollable sexual urges that "good" women were supposed to hold in check. Men pursue while women hold out for commitment, intimacy, and marriage. The assumption that it is OK for men to try and "get it" by any means necessary—including lying about caring for the woman, getting her drunk, just about anything short of rape—is accepted and explicit. Men bragging about their "conquests" is a given. Unethical sexual behavior is justified because it is assumed that men's sexual "urges" are so overwhelming that they simply cannot help themselves. Lying, cheating, hurting others' feelings are just part of a funny game. This leaves poor Doris with the thankless job of refusing sex, all the while keeping the man interested until she can force/trick/coerce him into a higher standard of behavior, usually involving personal commitment and marriage. Good/smart/pretty girls find creative ways to get men to delay their gratification, holding their sexual energy until it can be brought into alignment with the "higher" social values of a caring, permanent relationship. It is never exactly clear whether Doris has any sexual desire; if she does it's a kind of passive, extremely romantic, fainting sort of desire that puts her at risk for being swept away with uncontrollable passion, but that can't happen because then she'd be a bad girl. Much of the plot involves watching Doris find ways of convincing or tricking men into thinking she is worth the restraints on their sexual desire and the potential boredom of marriage and commitment. Things have changed.

The New Female Rat Pack: Power Without the Fun

Many girls are now pursuing sex without intimacy and boasting to their friends over their "conquests" in a way that would make Dean Martin blush. They've taken on the aggressive swagger of the infamous "rat pack" of that era. Are we to assume our daughters have achieved some sort of equality? They can certainly do anything the boys can do. (Although the word "slut" can still be brought in to skewer a girl's reputation seemingly on a whim. Confusingly, the exact same behavior in a different time and place will be applauded, and viewed as a source of power and prestige.) Girls have now acquired the freedom to use sex as a form of power and manipulation, just like the boys. But there is one huge distinction. When Dean Martin manipulated some inebriated female into giving it up, and later bragged about it to Frank, he was boasting about being able to achieve release of sexual energy without consequences. Girls today are bragging, but it's about *giving* sexual release, not getting it.[1] The pleasure part of the sexual event is completely one-sided. I have rarely seen a teenage girl and never seen a preteen in my office, workshop, or class who pursued or acquiesced to sexual relations for the purpose of sexual release. Most have never had an orgasm and don't really know what it involves. On the contrary, most have found oral sex and sexual intercourse unpleasant, if not "gross." The sexual revolution, as being expressed by many girls in middle school, high school, and to some extent college, is not about the free giving and receiving of sexual pleasure. For the girl, most often it's not about pleasure at all. It is about having the power to attract the boys, pleasure the boys, and dump the boys.

Time-out for a Little *Sex and the City*

If girls today aren't expecting sexual satisfaction one certainly can't fault those iconic women on *Sex and the City.*[2] Completely fulfilling the fantasy that women can and should express their sexuality just like men, Carrie, Amanda, Miranda, and Charlotte did their best to educate a generation of women about the ways of attaining sexual pleasure. Not only did women have a right to sexual pleasure, they could initiate it, explore it without intimacy, and best of all, have a great time discussing it with their bff's (best friends forever). Expressing their right to sex without intimacy, they did the male rat pack of the 1940s one better. Frank and Dean got their sexual desires met but lived life quite devoid of intimacy. The ladies in the *City* not only demanded sexual satisfaction, but also got to have intimacy, with their girlfriends.

College girls I see in my practice tell me that girls like to imagine themselves as capable of the same aggressive sexuality as these gorgeous New York women, but that it usually doesn't work.

Jessica is in her senior year of college and, after many hookups, has come into therapy to "figure out the guy thing."

"Lots of girls think it's supposed to be like *Sex and the City*: find a hot guy, hook up, and move on. But when we sit around and talk, I mean with my close friends, it's mostly about whether or not we're going to hear from him again."

A 2001 study of sexual attitudes of college women reinforces this dissatisfaction. "While hooking up is portrayed by some students as a bold move made by a modern woman, it is interesting to note how often these women ended up in a distinctly vulnerable position, waiting by the phone for the guy to call, and allowing the guy to define the status of the relationship."[3] As Carrie Bradshaw might ask:

> Is it true that women care more about intimacy than men do? Just because women can have sex without intimacy, does that mean they want to?

Sex and the City Goes to Middle School, with a Difference

Week after week, the women from *The City* take their sexual desire; get dressed up in hot, expensive clothes; go to a club, attract a guy, bring him home, and have satisfying sex, which they spend the second half of the show discussing with their friends. In middle school, girls have got the hot clothes and the how-to-attract-a-guy part down, they've figured out how to *use* their power, but that's where the similarity ends. Unlike Carrie Bradshaw, these girls are giving sexual pleasure but not receiving it. There's no satisfying sexual release at the end of their story. Middle school girls are just experiencing the first twinges of sexual desire and have no clear idea about how to get those desires met. But amazingly, they are well versed in the techniques necessary to service the desires of the boys. So what happens when girls start prematurely playing with their power?

Time: 2004

Place: Massachusetts Private School

A fifteen-year-old girl, apparently of her own free will, has oral sex with a group of boys in the boys' locker room. Because this takes place in a prestigious private institution that for some unfathomable reason cannot keep a lid on the story, the details of the event are repeated over and over on talk radio and TV for weeks, in an endless blather of sanctimonious outrage and tasteless jokes. In the end, the boys are expelled. More outrage. Parents call me wondering if this kind of behavior is really as common as the media seems to be suggesting. Yes. Are their sons at risk legally if the girl is the one doing the pursuing? Yes.

All the while I am wondering what would have happened if a fifteen-year-old boy had been caught having oral sex with a group of girls. And why was it so hard to even imagine that? One particularly vile talk show host sticks in my mind: "What kind of boy would refuse a girl who was offering oral sex!" he repeated over and over. Implying that any boy who did not willingly agree to stick his penis in a girl's mouth that he had no particular relationship with, in front of an audience, would undoubtedly have to be gay. What amazed me most was that none of the teens I talked with about this incident could understand what the big deal was. Why would anyone care? Stuff happens.

The more I talked with teens, parents, teachers, health professionals, and the media about this incident, the more it seemed to be a snapshot of our time, an event that captured so much of what has changed and what has stayed the same about how we think about sex. As adults, our inclination was to see this girl as a victim of peer pressure. Why else would she have put herself in this position? Teens I spoke with did not agree.

Ben (age seventeen): "Why does it always have to be the guy's fault? That's totally wack. Plenty of girls ask guys if they want, you know, blow jobs. When I was in eighth grade a girl sent me a note saying 'blow job or hand job?' I didn't even know her."

Nora (age twenty-two): "Sometimes it's not so clear. When you're young, you can get messed up thinking that people will like you if you do stupid shit. But it was still her choice."

Joan (age fifteen): "I'm not saying it's the guy's fault, but it's pretty disgusting. She was a slut and they could have said no."

Lenny (age sixteen): "I don't know what kind of pressure was on the girl, but if one of those guys had said no the other guys really would have given him shit about being gay."

Teens did not assume that the girl was the victim. They live in a world where they can imagine a girl initiating this behavior as a way to acquire bragging rights. And although it was clear that she had risked being labeled a slut, that word did not have the permanent, negative association it had in her parents' generation. ("Slut" can also be used as a term of teasing endearment.) All parties involved were seen as having equal responsibility. If anything, the boys were seen as perhaps under more peer pressure, as refusal to participate would have made them fair game to be characterized as something far more damning in the world of teenage boys than a slut.

What About the Boys?

What happens to a twelve-year-old boy when a girl offers him a blow job?

Let's hope he's not living in the macho land of the talk show host, the good ole boy world where real men have unrelenting sexual desire. If that's his reality, he'd better jump at the opportunity, like it or not, because in that world, refusing sex is immediately suspect. He must be gay.[4]

If girls are becoming more aggressive sexually, where does that leave boys? Raised in a culture where they've been supported for being the pursuer, what happens when they become the pursued? If a girl initiates sex, can a boy say no? Certainly younger boys, middle school kids, are apt to be teased or labeled gay. By college, many boys are simply enjoying the increased opportunities for sex but many are just anxious.

In my private practice, as confused and disconnected as the girls are, the boys seem even more confused. Trying to figure out what masculine means when girls have usurped a great deal of their "masculine" territory can be overwhelming and demoralizing. Many boys, caught in the demands of the hookup scene, quietly long for relationship. Some are taking Viagra.

"Do you think it would be OK if I started taking Viagra?" Ethan, a nineteen-year-old college freshman, is not cutting it in the world of hooking up. Although sexually active in high school with a girlfriend for more than a year, Ethan has twice failed to sustain an erection in college. He is terrified that the girls in his dorm are all talking about him. The first girl had approached him at a sorority party. They were both drunk and she wanted to "do it" in the bathroom. The second time, he was part of a booty call. A group of girls on another floor had contacted him and his two roommates online. A booty call is an invitation to sex, not necessarily intercourse, but some sort of hooking up. Being part of a booty call is both flattering and exciting. But for a freshman boy who is not excited by the idea of recreational sex, it can be terrifying. Failing again to achieve an erection, Ethan is convinced his reputation is ruined and that he must do something extreme to turn things around. Many heterosexual college and high school boys I see in my private practice are struggling to hold a view of sexuality that says they're not crazy, gay, or impotent if they don't want to engage in sex without intimacy. Unlike the girls who tend to blame the boys for the way things are, the boys are more likely to feel that there is just something wrong with them.

During This Time of Transition

None of us knows where sexuality is headed. Many of us don't even know where we want it to go. As a species, we've never had to figure out what to do with our sexuality as single people for such a long period of our lives.

Women, with opportunities for higher education, financial independence, and without fear of unwanted pregnancy, have been exploring sexual "freedom" since the sixties. But what does freedom mean? In many ways for girls today, freedom is just a less satisfying, rehashed version of what males defined as freedom in the forties and fifties. And who's to say that men ever knew what sexual freedom meant. Turning sex into a commodity to be acquired and bragged about isn't freedom. Relentlessly pursuing pleasure is an addiction, the furthest thing from freedom.

There has never been a time when males and females entered the sexual arena so close to a level playing field as exists for college men and women today. In their hands exists the opportunity to create something new that engages the best of male and female sexuality. Trying to figure it out will continue to be excruciatingly confusing. Author Barrett Seaman, who has chronicled the excesses of college life, puts it this way:

"Perhaps someday society will reach a higher plane of gender equality, but at this juncture of our cultural evolution, young men and women remain caught between old traditions and new expectations. The tectonic plates are rubbing up against one another. . . ."[5]

Why should our kids have to figure it out alone? We can teach our daughters that real sexual freedom means expecting mutual sexual satisfaction. We can teach our sons that real men can choose intimacy and relationship. We can hold on to what is beautiful and sacred about our religious traditions and enrich what we teach our children by being open to learning from other traditions.

What If We Were Really Free?

I'm not sure I can fully grasp what gender equality and true sexual freedom would look like. I do know it should not be confused with both sexes being "free" to do anything they want based on their most immediate desire. There's no freedom in excess; there is only more need. I do know that we could save our children a great deal of pain if we would take the time to start a dialogue. Giving them a language to understand the power of sexual desire, helping them develop the muscle of self-discipline, inspiring them with the mystery of love and relationship are gifts we can afford to give.

epilogue

∙∙∙∙∙∙∙∙∙∙∙∙∙∙∙∙∙∙∙∙∙

there are moms and dads who wake up in the wee hours of the morning, day after day, and do whatever is necessary to make sure their children have the best chance possible of growing into healthy, responsible, and successful adults. And after working all day and arranging child care at night, they come to a talk given by someone like me because they really want to understand how they can do the job of parenting just a little bit better. These parents are under siege. They work all the time just to keep things going and are expected to do parenting in the time they have left. A sick child, a bout of the flu, the loss of a job, a kid in trouble at school, anything can push the stress over the top and send the whole precarious structure into free fall. Extended families, religious institutions, neighborhoods; the structures that help us raise our children and care for each other are so often missing, replaced by the characters on favorite television shows, Oprah, overworked teachers, and the mall.

We can't raise a generation of sexually healthy adults in our spare time, by ourselves, and we can't go back in time. But we can look at the factors that support community and family, and start thinking about how we can bring those factors into the lives we have now. We can beg our leaders to stop polarizing us by competing to see who has the best "family values," and start legislating in a manner that protects the time we need with our children; time to bond with them when they're first born, nurse them when they're sick, protect them from corporations who abuse them for profit, and be there to listen when they need answers to the questions that will define them.

I thank every parent who has ever come up to me after a talk and told me their story or thanked me for giving them a new way of thinking about things that ended up helping them parent their kids. Your love and commitment are inspiring. Your stories inform my thinking. When I say good night to my own children, in that precious moment of love and gratitude that comes from being given the gift to do this job at all, I imagine parents everywhere looking at their kids and praying so fervently that they are up to the job. I sometimes imagine what we might accomplish if we took the power of the love we feel for our children and made children in this country a priority and parenting a doable job.

SHARON MAXWELL, PH.D.
DrSharonMaxwell.com

appendix 1

. . . .

Contract for Safety

By signing this contract for safety I understand each of the sentences written below and agree to all the terms of this contract.

teen agreement

1. I understand that drinking alcohol or doing drugs interferes with my brain's ability to think clearly and make intelligent choices.
2. These choices can involve taking unsafe risks, like driving a car, or getting in a car without assessing whether or not the driver has been drinking, or getting involved in sexual situations that are unsafe.
3. I understand that drinking or doing drugs prevents people from driving safely EVEN IF THEY'VE ONLY HAD ONE DRINK.
4. I will never drive if I have used ANY alcohol or drugs.
5. I will never get in a car if the person driving has taken ANY alcohol or drugs.
6. I know how to assess whether or not someone has been drinking or doing drugs.

7. If I am ever in a situation where I feel as if I am un-safe whether because I have taken drugs or alcohol or the people I am with have taken drugs or alcohol, I will call you.

8. If I am ever in a situation where I am unsure whether the people responsible for driving me home have taken drugs or alcohol, I will call you.

*(teen signature)*_____

parent agreement

1. You can call me AT ANY TIME, should you feel unsafe, FOR ANY REASON, and I will come and get you.

2. I will NOT ASK ANY QUESTIONS when I pick you up.

3. I will NOT PUNISH YOU IN ANY WAY.

*(parent signature)*_____

appendix 2

....

Sample Guidelines for Responsible Online Behavior

(Parents: Use this as a starting point for discussion. Your guidelines may be different and will change as your child demonstrates responsible behavior.)

Having access to the Internet is a privilege that we earn by using the Internet in a responsible manner. These guidelines reflect our family values. If any of us has a problem with these guidelines we will discuss our concerns honestly and with an open mind.

1. I will access parent-approved sites only.
2. I will not open any e-mail unless I know whom it is from.
3. I will give my parents a copy of all my passwords.
4. I will not communicate with people I do not know.
5. I will never give out personal information to anyone on-line, and I will inform my parents if anyone asks for this information (name, address, phone number, school, or e-mail address).
6. I understand that what I say matters and I will *not*:

- Use words in any form to harm or threaten, intimidate, or bully anyone.
- Start or spread gossip.
- Use curse words or obscene language, even in abbreviated Internet language.
- I will be careful about "fooling around" and will never say that I will do something I really don't want to do.

7. I understand that some online behaviors can become addictive. I will be conscious of how much time I am spending online and will try to balance my time.
8. I understand that everything I see and read online is not necessarily true and that it is my responsibility to figure out what is true and what is not.
9. I understand that my right to privacy online depends on how responsibly I use the Internet. My parents maintain the right to review my e-mails, IM conversations, Web pages, and all browser history files.

appendix 3

....

Taking Control of Our Time

In the best of all possible worlds, how would you like your child to spend his or her time? What kind of schedule nurtures a healthy, balanced, responsible life?

Take time with your partner to look at the list of activities below and rank them according to what you value most. You don't have to agree, and some activities may have equal value.

Imagine that the circle on page 204 is the amount of time your child has in a week. Divide up the circle into slices, giving each activity the amount of time you think would be best. Feel free to add or subtract from the list.

Compare this ideal week to the average week your child is living now (see page 172).

- Time in nature
- Physical activity (sports, dance)
- Time with peers
- Time with family
- One-on-one mommy/daddy time
- Silence
- Spiritual practice/education
- Listening to music

- Lessons (music, art, theater)
- Sleep
- Interactive media (Internet, games)
- Passive media (TV, movies)
- Time with extended family
- Alone time
- Fantasy playtime
- Reading
- Shopping
- Eating/food preparation
- Community service

appendix 4

∙∙∙∙∙∙∙∙∙∙∙∙∙∙∙∙∙∙∙∙∙∙

Eleven Principles
for Sexual Behavior

1. Your body, and the decision about how to use it, belongs only to you. Anyone who tries to force or manipulate you into having sex of any kind does not respect himself or herself, and does not respect you.

2. How you choose to use your body and how you choose not to use your body become part of who you are. The choices you make today tell you and the rest of the world what you're about and, more important, how you see yourself physically, emotionally, and spiritually.

3. Any kind of sexual behavior that involves another person is an expression of intimacy. The more sexual you choose to be with someone, the more you are choosing to share who you really are.

4. Being sexual with someone can be fun and playful, but it is always personal and private. Sex is never a spectator sport.

5. Choosing to express your sexuality is a conscious act. Allowing it to "just happen" or engaging in sex when you are less than fully conscious is dangerous and diminishes your ability to give it the consideration it deserves.

6. Letting someone know your body and exploring some-

one else's body is an amazing experience. It should only be done with someone you respect and trust. Sex should never be used to gain power, popularity, or as a cure for loneliness.

7. Before you let anyone know you body, make sure they have shown you that they care enough to want to really know you.

8. Before you invite someone to really know you in an intimate way, spend time getting to know yourself. As you better understand who you are, what you believe in, and what you care about, you begin to be ready to share yourself with someone else.

9. Never pretend to care about someone as a way to get him or her to be sexual with you.

10. Being sexual with someone should feel good. It should never be painful, disgusting, or humiliating.

11. Sex is always a two-way street. If the person you're with only cares about their own pleasure, they don't really care about you.

notes

●●●●●●●●●●●●●●●●●●

chapter one

1. Although unable to confirm this with 3D Realms, I have confirmed similar content in Duke Nukem and have no reason to believe this mother was not accurate in her understanding of the game.
2. Joseph Gelmis, "Shoot to Thrill or Shoot to Kill?: The Littleton Massacre Has Reopened the Debate about Violent Video Games. A Video Age," *Newsday*, May 11, 1999, p. B06.
3. Bruce Horovitz, "Six Strategies Marketers Use to Get Kids to Want Stuff Bad," *USA Today*, November 22, 2006, p. B1.
4. Katy Kelly and Linda Kulman, "Kid Power," *U.S. News and World Report*, Sept. 13, 2004, www.usnews.com/usnews/culture/articles/040913/13kids_2.htm; p. 2.
5. Wayne Chilicki, General Mills executive, as quoted in "Directing the Pitch: Do Smart Marketers to Children Target Kids or Their Parents?" *Youth Markets Alert*, July 1, 1998, p. 3.
6. Task Force on Advertising and Children, American Psychological Association, 2000, www.apa.org/releases/childrenads.pdf
7. Ron Harris, "Children Who Dress for Excess: Today's Youngsters Have Become Fixated with Fashion. The Right Look Isn't Enough—It Also Has to Be Expensive," *Los Angeles Times*, Nov. 12, 1989, p. A1.
8. Donald F. Roberts, Ulla G. Foehr, and Victoria Rideout, "Generation M: Media in the Lives of 8–18-Year-Olds," Kaiser Family Foundation Report, March 2005, www.kff.org/entmedia/upload/Generation-M-Media-in-the-Lives-of-8-18-Year-Olds-Report.pdf
9. "Merchants of Cool," *Frontline*, Public Broadcasting Service, aired February 27, 2001.
10. U.S. Census Bureau, *Current Population Survey*, Annual Social and Economical Supplement, 2006.
11. National Center for Health Statistics, 2005; http://www.cdc.gov/nchs/fastats/divorce.htm

12. "The Lost Children of Rockdale County," *Frontline,* Public Broadcasting Service, aired October 19, 1999. Transcript available at www.pbs.org/wgbh/pages/frontline/shows/georgia/etc/script.html.
13. Report of the Task Force on the Sexualization of Girls, American Psychological Association, released Feb. 19, 2007. Tips on what parents can do to protect their daughters are available at www.apa.org/pi/wop/sexualizationpar.html.
14. Roberts et al., Kaiser Family Foundation Report, March 2005.
15. Benoit Denizet-Lewis, "Friends, Friends with Benefits and the Benefits of the Local Mall," *New York Times Magazine,* May 30, 2004, p. 30.
16. "Adolescents' Sexual Relationships: Boy/Girlfriends, Ex's, Friends, and Others," Department of Sociology and Center for Family and Demographic Research, Bowling Green State University, Ohio, April 1, 2004, www.bgsu.edu/organizations/cfdr/research/pdf/2005/2005-03.pdf
17. Carol Groneman, *Nymphomania: A History* (New York: W. W. Norton & Company, 2001), p. 143.
18. Stephen Buka, Sc.D., "Depressive Symptoms as a Longitudinal Predictor of Sexual Risk Behaviors Among U.S. Middle and High School Students," Jocelyn Lehrer, Sc.D., Lidia Shrier, M.D., MPH, Steven Grotmaker, Ph.D., and *Pediatrics,* Vol. 118, no. 1, 2006, pp. 189–200.

chapter two
1. This certainly does not apply to all dance recitals, but parents are strongly urged to attend a recital before signing their child up for dance classes.
2. Peter Mayle, *Where Did I Come From?* (New York: Citadel-Kensington, 1977).

chapter three
1. Eddy Ramirez, "Students Say Bus Driver Ignored Sexual Behavior," *St. Petersburg Times,* March 9, 2007, p. 1.
2. One mom received diaper covers that said "Juicy" as a shower gift for her unborn daughter.
3. "The Critical Years: Challenge of Middle School," *The New York Times,* Jan. 22, 2007 (three-part series and online video on January 3, January 22, and March 17, 2007, in New York region. Reported and produced by Elissa Goatman, Shayla Harris, and Adam Ellick), video.on.nytime.com

4. CW network combines Warner Brothers and UPN television networks to target 18- to 34-year-old viewers, Fall 2006.

chapter four

1. *Spider-Man*, Columbia Pictures Corporation, 2002.
2. Centers for Disease Control and Prevention; www.cdc.gov/std/default .htm
3. *Everybody Is Talking to Your Child About Sex. What Are They Hearing from You?* Norfolk County District Attorney, Massachusetts, 2003, http://www.mass.gov/da/norfolk/PDF%20Brochures/Teen%20Sex %20Booklet%20to%20Parents.pdf
4. Diane Zuckerman, Ph.D., "Research on Teen Suicide," The National Research Center for Children and Families, Washington, D.C., June 2005, http://www.center4research.org/suicide.html
5. Helpful resources include the Parents, Families and Friends of Lesbians and Gays Web site, at www.pflag.org. Also check out "Just the Facts about Sexual Orientation & Youth: A Primer for Principals, Educators & School Personnel," by the American Psychological Association; at www.apa.org/pi/online.html#LGB

chapter five

1. *Sex and Drugs*, The National Campaign to End Teen Pregnancy, 1/2/2003, teenpregnancy.org

chapter six

1. Princeton Survey Research Associates for the Henry J. Kaiser Family Foundation (June 1996), *The 1996 Kaiser Family Foundation Survey on Teens and Sex: What Teens Today Say They Need to Know, and Who They Listen To,* Menlo Park, California.
2. Taken from an improvisational exercise from the Sexual Health and Responsibility curriculum, Dr. Sharon Maxwell, © 2002.
3. Barrett Seaman, *Binge: Campus Life in an Age of Disconnection and Excess* (Hoboken, NJ: John Wiley & Sons, Inc., 2005), p. 41.
4. National Highway Traffic and Safety Administration, 2003; www .nhtsa.gov
5. Mothers Against Drunk Driving; http://www.madd.org/aboutus/ 1211

chapter seven

1. Robie H. Harris and Michael Emberley, *It's Perfectly Normal: Changing Bodies, Growing Up, Sex, and Sexual Health* (Cambridge, MA: Candlewick Press, 2004).
2. David Walsh, Ph.D., *Why Do They Act That Way?* (New York: Free Press, 2004), p. 7.
3. Jay N. Giedd, Jonathan Blumenthal, Neal O. Jefferies, F. X. Castellanos, Hong Liu, Alex Zijdenbos, Tomas Paus, Alan C. Evans, and Judith L. Rapoport, "Brain development during childhood and adolescence: a longitudinal MRI study," *Nature Neuroscience* 2 (1999): 861–63.
4. H. Nevil, J. Mehler, E. Newpert, J. Werker, and J. McClelland, 2001 *Language* Special Issue: The Developing Human Brain, Developmental Science 4(3), pp. 293–312.
5. Barbara Strauch, *The Primal Teen: What the New Discoveries About the Teenage Brain Tell Us About Our Kids*, New York: Anchor Books/Random House, 2003, p. 17.
6. Time-Lapse Imaging Tracks Brain Maturation from Ages 5 to 20, Paul Thompson, Ph.D., USCL Laboratory of Neuroimaging, http://www.nimh.nih.gov/science-news/2004/imaging-study-shows-brain-maturing.shtml
7. Giedd et al., 861–63.
8. Deborah Yurgelun-Todd cited in "Inside the Teenage Brain. One Reason Teens Respond Differently to the World: Immature Brain Circuitry"; http://www.pbs.org/wgbh/pages/frontline/shows/teenbrain/work/onereason.html

chapter eight

1. "The Lost Children of Rockdale County," *Frontline,* Public Broadcasting Service, aired October 19, 1999.
2. *Middle Sexes: Redefining He and She,* an HBO documentary, 2005.

chapter ten

1. Task Force on the Sexualization of Girls, American Psychological Association, February 19, 2001.
2. http://www.timeforkids.com/TFK/kids/news/story/0,28277,1006625,00.html
3. lsafe.org: fbi.gov/publications/pguide/pguide.htm
4. "Merchants of Cool," *Frontline*, Public Broadcasting Service, aired February 27, 2001.

chapter eleven

1. "The Lost Children of Rockdale County," *Frontline,* Public Broadcasting Service, aired October 19, 1999.
2. *Sex and the City,* HBO.
3. "Hooking Up, Hanging Out and Hoping for Mr. Right: College Women on Mating and Dating Today," an Institute for American Values Report to the Independent Women's Forum, Norval Glenn, professor of sociology, University of Texas, and Elizabeth Marquardt, affiliate scholar at the Institute for American Values, July 2001, p. 19.
4. Barbara Meltz, "Boys Can Have Bad Reputations, Too," *The Boston Globe,* April 3, 2003, p. H3.
5. Seaman, *Binge,* p. 50.

index

. . . .

online sexual identity, *(cont.)*
  and shy kids, 163–165
  social networking sites, 162–163
  talking online, 170–171
opposing roles, 87
Oprah Winfrey Show, The
  (TV show), 175
oral sex, 10, 190–192
orgasm, 59, 188
overgeneralizations, 126
ownership, feelings of, 157

parents
  as best resource for teens, 117
  birthing teens into adulthood,
    81–82
  cluelessness of, 3
  conflict with teens, 86–88
  creating structure teens can
    push against, 89–91
  derailed by teen attitude, 84–86
  dialogue changes with teens,
    79–80
  doing your job, 96–98
  emotional roller-coaster ride of,
    102–103
  explaining biology of sex,
    25–30
  guarding portal to Internet,
    168–169
  immigrant, 166–167
  isolation from other parents,
    175–176
  making connections with others,
    176–178
  preparing teens for sexual
    power, 49–51
  protecting children from sexual
    abuse, 47–49
  questions about assessing teen's
    maturity, 92–93
  questions about changes in teen,
    131–132

questions about desires and
  control, 47
questions about disagreeing
  with teens, 88–89
questions about emotional coping, 116–117
questions about excess online
  stimulation, 172–173
questions about explaining biology of sex, 28–29, 31
questions about lust vs. love,
  158
questions about media manipulation, 8, 114
questions about religion and
  sexuality, 146
questions about sexual behavior, 19
questions about sexual behavior
  guidelines, 150
questions about "sexy," 39
questions about structure,
  103–104
questions about teen brain,
  129–130
questions about teen support
  systems, 120
questions about the Internet,
  179
questions about the sexuality
  continuum, 153–154
questions about underage sex,
  58
setting boundaries for sexual
  behavior, 22–23
talking about love, 154–155
talking about "sexy," sexual
  desire, and reproduction,
  41–42
talking with teens, 88
telling daughters how world
  "works," 55
partying, 77

about the author

· ·

Sharon Maxwell, Ph.D., has been a practicing clinical psychologist for seventeen years. Specializing in adolescent sexuality, she is a frequent lecturer on issues of sex and sexuality, teen Internet use, how mothers can guide their daughters through puberty, and how parents can create a value-filled family culture to help kids navigate media and peer pressure. Dr. Maxwell won a national award from Parenting Publications of America for her series of articles on sex education and has received recognition for the success of her sexual health and responsibility curriculum, which is being used in both public and private schools. Dr. Maxwell works with religious educators from different traditions, providing workshops for parents and teens that incorporate her perspective on sexuality and sexual ethics. The Commonwealth of Massachusetts features her work in brochures on sex education and in a DVD on teens and drunk driving. Maxwell is the mother of two teens and lives near Boston with her family. For more information, please visit her website at www .drsharonmaxwell.com.